Kit Beginning Reader Books

Level C: Kit Is Reading Now

Written by Max Loony

This volume contains all 5 books in Level C:
- Book C-1: Kit Explores A House
- Book C-2: Kit Goes Out To Eat
- Book C-3: Kit Explores The Earth
- Book C-4: Kit Loves Life!
- Book C-5: Kit Goes Home!

All of the included books in this volume are written using *only* words up to 5 letters long! The full edition of each of these 5 paperback books is included: cover illustrations, inside cover "at a glance" views of the concepts covered in each book, and alphabetized lists of all words at the end of each.

Download free parent/teacher guide at:
readiculousbooks.com/kit

Copyright © 2023 Read-iculous Books

All rights reserved. Reproduction of this work, in whole or in part, in any manner whatsoever, is strictly prohibited, except for brief quotations embodied in critical articles and reviews.

ISBN: 9798395026163

Kit Explores A House

An Easy-Start Reader

Level C, Book 1

by
Max Loony

READ-ICULOUS BOOKS

Kit Beginning Reader Books

Level C: Kit Is Reading Now

Book C-1: Kit Explores A House

Written by Max Loony

Concepts in this book*:
- Introduction to 5-letter words with simple rhyme schemes
- Only short words (1-5 letters)
- Short vowel sounds in patterns CCVCC, CVCCC, CCCVC, and *qu*VCC
- Long vowel sounds in patterns CCVCe and *qu*VCe
- One-syllable short vowel sounds in patterns CVCCs, CVVCs, and CCVCs
- One-syllable long vowel sounds in patterns CVCes, CVVCs, and CCVVs
- Vowel combination (*ea*) in pattern —C*ea*C—
- Long double-vowel sound (*ee*) in pattern —C*ee*C—
- Double-vowel sound (*oo*) making 2 different sounds in pattern —C*oo*C—
- Vowel-consonant combo (*ow*) making 2 different sounds in pattern —*ow*—
- Vowel-consonant ending exception sound (—*ink*)
- Strong "s" sound in ending patterns —*ce*, —*se*, and —*sks*
- A few new two- and three-consonant blends (—*rl*, *scr*—, *sm*—, *wr*—)
- Several new two-syllable words including new patterns *a*CVCC, CVCVC, and CVCC*y*
- Introduction to 5-letter three-syllable word in pattern VCVVC (*alien*)
- Introduction to acronyms (*TV*)
- Several new phonetic exceptions (*girl, girls, floor, there, were, where*)

*Word Pattern Key: C=Consonant, V=Vowel, *italics*=a specific letter, —(dash)=start or end of word

Download free parent/teacher guide at:
     readiculousbooks.com/kit

Copyright © 2023 Read-iculous Books

All rights reserved. Reproduction of this work, in whole or in part, in any manner whatsoever, is strictly prohibited, except for brief quotations embodied in critical articles and reviews.

BOOK C-1: KIT EXPLORES A HOUSE

by Max Loony

It is such a nice day!
Well, I just have to say
That I think I will walk to the town!

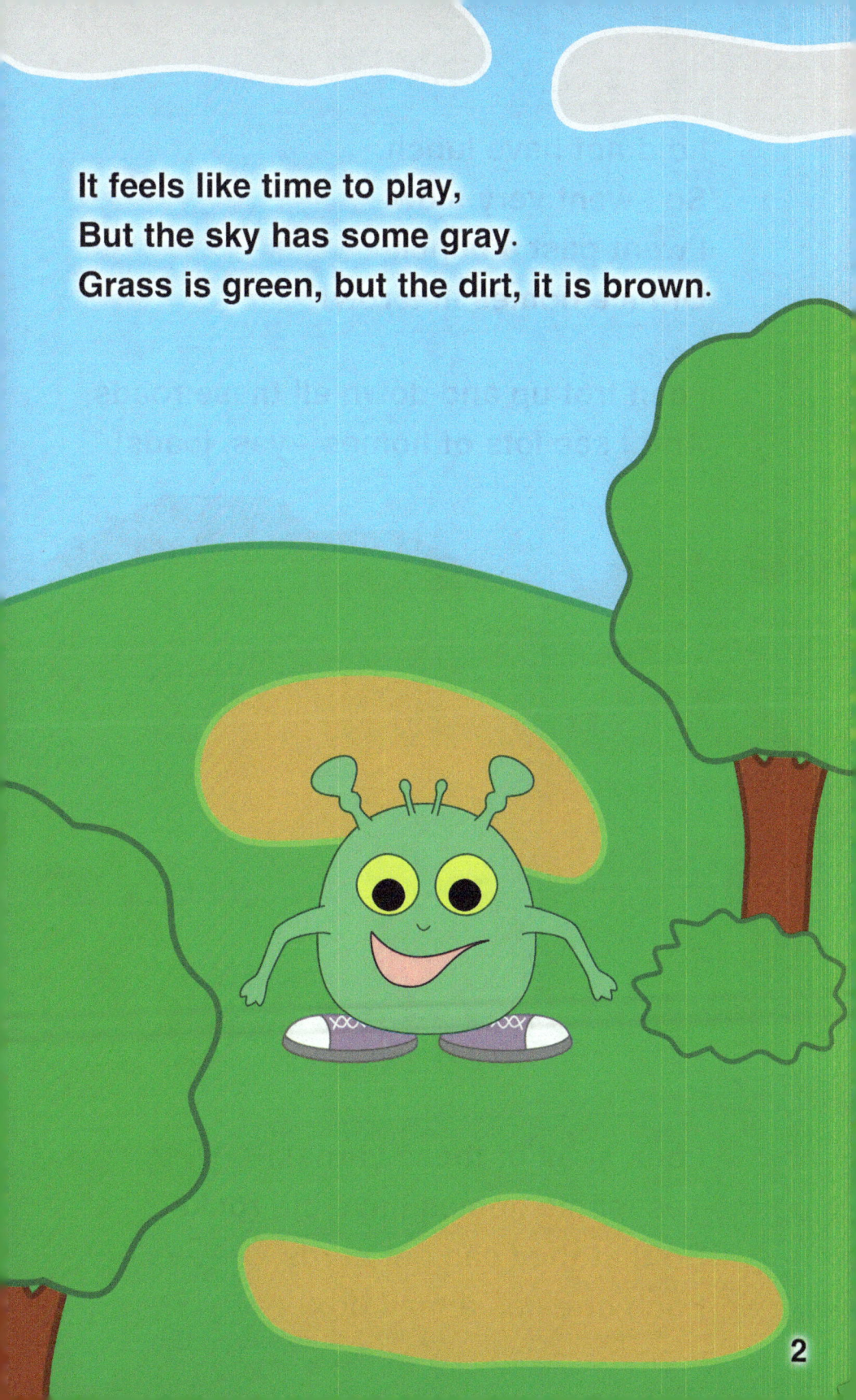

It feels like time to play,
But the sky has some gray.
Grass is green, but the dirt, it is brown.

I did not have lunch,
So I went very slow.
I went past a bunch
Of nice homes in a row!

I can trot up and down all these roads,
And I see lots of homes—yes, loads!

Look at all of these yards!
Yes, some homes have big rocks!
So that they can get cards,
Each one has a mail box!

And some yards have big holes.
Some have flags up on poles.
Some have weeds, some have trees.
I mean, look at all these!
I can see in this zone,
Some have paths made of stone!

I came up to one home,
And I did stop my trot.
I said, I can still roam
Or else pause at this spot!

Hey, look where they park that big truck!
See those tires that are wide?
There are two on each side,
And they look just like they are stuck!

To my self I did chat,
For I, Kit, am like that!

What kind of stuff is kept in a house?
What if in the walls is a mouse?

I'll see what I can find
While I am out on this walk,
And I sure will not mind
To meet a human and talk!

I saw that the front door was wide open
On this house as I did walk along.
So I said, "What if I just go in?"
You see, I did not know it was wrong!

Then I, Kit, went on in
With my big silly grin!
Then a man and a woman saw me.

They said, "Hey, who are you?
Tell us now and be true!"
So I told them what I came to see.

I said, "I'd like to know
What you keep in this house.
How does life in here flow,
And do you have a mouse?

What stuff can I feel, and what can I smell?
What thing can I see, and what can I hold?
If I can find out, then that will be swell!"
I did ask them this, for I was quite bold!

"Where did you come from?" They did ask.
So to tell them was now my task.
Then I said, "I'm from way out in space!
My name is Kit, and I like this place!"

So they said, "Well, okay.
Our place is quite messy,
But we will let you look at our home.

You can now go and play!"
And I was so happy
That I, Kit, was now free to just roam.

Since each room had a door,
I went in all of them to see more.
When I saw each new thing,
I, Kit, felt like I just want to sing!

13

In one room were some books
And two capes hung on hooks.
On a desk were some dimes and a penny,

A few bucks and some rings,
And a doll that had wings.
Oh, the dolls! There sure were so many!

And I saw there were vents
Way high up in the walls
So that each of the rooms can get air.

I said, "Well, that makes sense,
But look there at those balls.
Now I ask: Is this next room a spare?"

On the side of this room
I did see a long broom
And a bunch of odd stuff on the floor.
So I left it to go see some more!

Some walls are brown, some white,
    and some green.
Some rooms are messy, but some
    are all clean!

In the next, I did see
It's a room with TV!
Is that some kind of show?
I don't care! Now, where else can I go?

Then I was in a hall,
And here is what I saw:
A big clock that was hung on the wall!

What else is in this place?
On a shelf way up high,
A plant and a glass vase
Were so near to the roof
That I need no more proof
Of a human much more tall than I!

"What else can I find here?"
I did ask with good cheer.

I came into a huge room for tasks,
And now these are the words that Kit asks:

What are those? Are they tools?
Also what are the rules
For all of the stuff that is here?
Is this even safe to be near?

I see a knife and a screw
And lots of trash, that is true,
And notes that were left on a paper.

Here some guy wrote a chart.
It's sure not the best art!
It looks like some plans to do later.

21

Wow, this place is a mess!
Now I wish I'd seen less,
So I left that room in a hurry!

To get this chore all done
Looks like weeks of no fun,
But it's not my task, so don't worry!

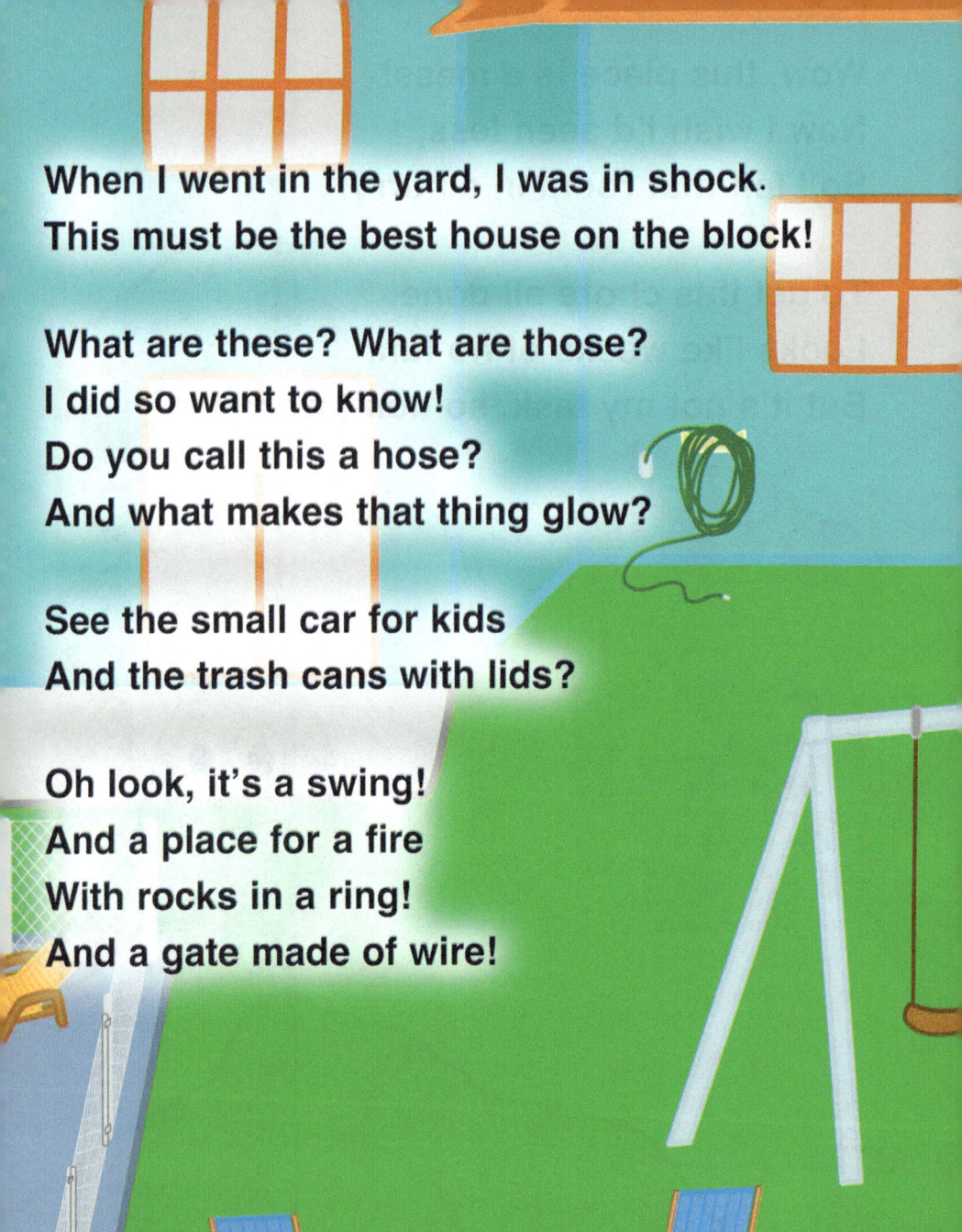

When I went in the yard, I was in shock.
This must be the best house on the block!

What are these? What are those?
I did so want to know!
Do you call this a hose?
And what makes that thing glow?

See the small car for kids
And the trash cans with lids?

Oh look, it's a swing!
And a place for a fire
With rocks in a ring!
And a gate made of wire!

24

Well, at least they have good sense. See the pool? It's got a fence!

Then I said, "Hey, isn't that cool? It's a slide that goes into the pool!"

So what else was out back?
And what did I find there?
Two kids sat with a snack:
A small boy with a stick,
And a girl with long hair!
I went over there quick,
And then I got off track,
For I, Kit, and the girl, we did click!

And I said, "This is such a nice yard!
To keep it all this clean, is it hard?"

With me the girl did talk,
For at least a short while.
And she wrote with pink chalk,
Then at me she did smile!

Ah, this girl, she did have so much charm!
In my mind, there went off an alarm!

28

The girl did look at me when I said,
"Sugar and spice and stuff that is nice.
I hear that is what girls are made of!"
Well, she gave me a kiss on my head.
Then the girl held me close once or twice,
And now I think that I am in love!

Now the yard felt so sunny,
And I said she was funny,
For she had a good sense of humor.

I said, "You are a prize!
I've got stars in my eyes!
Check my head! Do I have a fever?"

We're from far apart lands,
But we sat and held hands.
Then the time came that we had to part.

Now the girl told me, "Bye!
I don't want you to cry!
Oh, dear Kit, it's okay,
For it's still a good day!"
And I saw that this girl was so smart!

For she is a human,
And I'm an alien.
So I just shook her hand,
And then I did stand,
And at last, on my way I did start.
But I still think her hair is like art!

Words in this book (new words are in **bold**):

1-letter words: a   I

2-letter words:

ah	do	is	oh	up
am	go	it	on	us
an	I'd	me	or	we
as	I'm	my	so	
at	if	no	to	
be	in	of	**TV**	

3-letter words:

air	car	has	now	sky
all	cry	her	odd	the
and	day	hey	off	two
are	did	how	one	was
art	far	I'll	our	way
ask	few	I've	out	who
big	for	it's	row	wow
box	fun	Kit	sat	yes
boy	get	let	saw	you
but	got	man	say	
bye	guy	new	see	
can	had	not	she	

4-letter words:

also	back	bold	came	care
asks	best	call	**cans**	chat

4-letter words (continued):

come	grin	**life**	play	time
cool	hair	like	**pool**	told
dear	hall	long	**ring**	town
desk	hand	look	roam	trot
dirt	**hard**	lots	roof	true
does	have	love	room	**vase**
doll	head	made	safe	very
don't	hear	mail	said	walk
done	**held**	many	seen	wall
door	here	mean	self	want
down	high	meet	show	we're
each	hold	mess	side	well
else	home	mind	sing	went
even	**hose**	more	slow	**were**
eyes	huge	much	some	what
feel	**hung**	must	spot	when
felt	into	name	stop	wide
find	isn't	near	such	will
fire	just	need	sure	**wire**
flow	keep	next	talk	wish
free	kept	nice	tall	with
from	kids	okay	task	**yard**
gate	kind	once	tell	zone
gave	**kiss**	open	than	
girl	know	over	that	
glow	last	park	them	
goes	left	part	then	
good	less	past	they	
gray	**lids**	**pink**	this	

34

5-letter words:

alarm	flags	paper	smell
alien	floor	paths	smile
along	front	pause	snack
apart	funny	penny	space
balls	girls	place	spare
block	glass	plans	spice
books	grass	plant	stand
broom	green	poles	stars
brown	hands	prize	start
bucks	happy	proof	stick
bunch	holes	quick	still
capes	homes	quite	stone
cards	hooks	rings	stuck
chalk	house	roads	stuff
charm	human	rocks	sugar
chart	humor	rooms	sunny
check	hurry	rules	swell
cheer	knife	screw	swing
chore	lands	sense	tasks
clean	later	shelf	there
click	least	shock	these
clock	loads	shook	thing
close	looks	short	think
dimes	lunch	silly	those
dolls	makes	since	tires
feels	messy	slide	tools
fence	mouse	small	track
fever	notes	smart	trash

5-letter words (continued):

trees	**weeds**	**wings**	**wrote**
truck	**weeks**	**woman**	**yards**
twice	**where**	**words**	
vents	**while**	**worry**	
walls	**white**	**wrong**	

Kit Goes Out To Eat

An Easy-Start Reader

Level C, Book 2

by
Max Loony

Kit Beginning Reader Books

Level C: Kit Is Reading Now

Book C-2: Kit Goes Out To Eat

Written by Max Loony

Concepts in this book*:
- Longer sentences and lengthier rhyme schemes
- Only short words (1-5 letters)
- Short vowel sounds in various previous patterns
- Long vowel sounds in various previous patterns
- Vowel combinations (*ai, oa, ui*) in patterns —C*ai*C—, —C*oa*C—, and —C*ui*C—
- Vowel combination (*ou*) making two different sounds in pattern —C*ou*C—
- Letter "c" pronounced as "s" when followed by "e", "i", or "y" in any pattern
- Second syllable consonant-vowel combo ending exception sound (—*le*)
- A few new two- and three-consonant blends (—*rth*, —*rv*—, *spl*—)
- Many new two-syllable words including new patterns aCVVC, aCCVV, aCVCV, VCCVC, VVCVC, CVCCV, CVCVV, CV*ing*, VCCC*y* CVC*ey*, and CCVC*y*
- Introduction to contractions using 5 letters (*didn't, that's, you'll, you're, you've*)
- Several new phonetic exceptions (*bread, comes, could, great, pizza, would*)

*Word Pattern Key: C=Consonant, V=Vowel, *italics*=a specific letter, —(dash)=start or end of word

Download free parent/teacher guide at:
　　　readiculousbooks.com/kit

Copyright © 2023 Read-iculous Books

All rights reserved. Reproduction of this work, in whole or in part, in any manner whatsoever, is strictly prohibited, except for brief quotations embodied in critical articles and reviews.

BOOK C-2: KIT GOES OUT TO EAT

by Max Loony

As I did walk along
By the shops in the day,
I sung an old song
While I went on my way.

Hey, I'd like some lunch!
Now where can I rest?
To get food that I'd munch,
Does this place pass the test?

Yes, that's all that I need—
Just a bite or two, tops!—
So that I can gain speed
When I'm back at the shops.

In the diner I went,
Then I did smell a scent.
I think it was a spice,
For it sure did smell nice!

At once, I was aware
Of music in the air.

I did not know the price
Of any food that they sold here.
I could pay for it, that much was clear!

When a lady saw me,
Her eyes grew wide as can be!
She did look at me twice.
Was it that I had no hair?
Was it okay that I was there?

At a table, I sat down.
It was flat and it was brown.

To me the woman came.
She wore a big apron.
On a tag was her name,
And her name was Susan.

Then she said, "Hey honey,
Do you have any money?"
So I said, "Yes, I do.
I've got gold, it is true."

She said, "Pick up the menu.
Take a look at it, then you
Tell me what you'd like to eat."

I took it out of its slot
And said, "What have you got?
Oh wow! This place sure looks neat!"

"Well, just what is your mood?
For our menu is split.
We have all kinds of food,
And we think you'll like it!"

But I, Kit, was slow,
And I said, "I don't know!"

"We've got food that is yummy!"
She said with a big smile.
"You'll like it in your tummy!"
But I still took a while.

By my table, she did stand.
With a menu in my hand,
She went over it all as she stood there.

She said, "Now take heed!
We have what you need!"
She went over each item with great care.

11

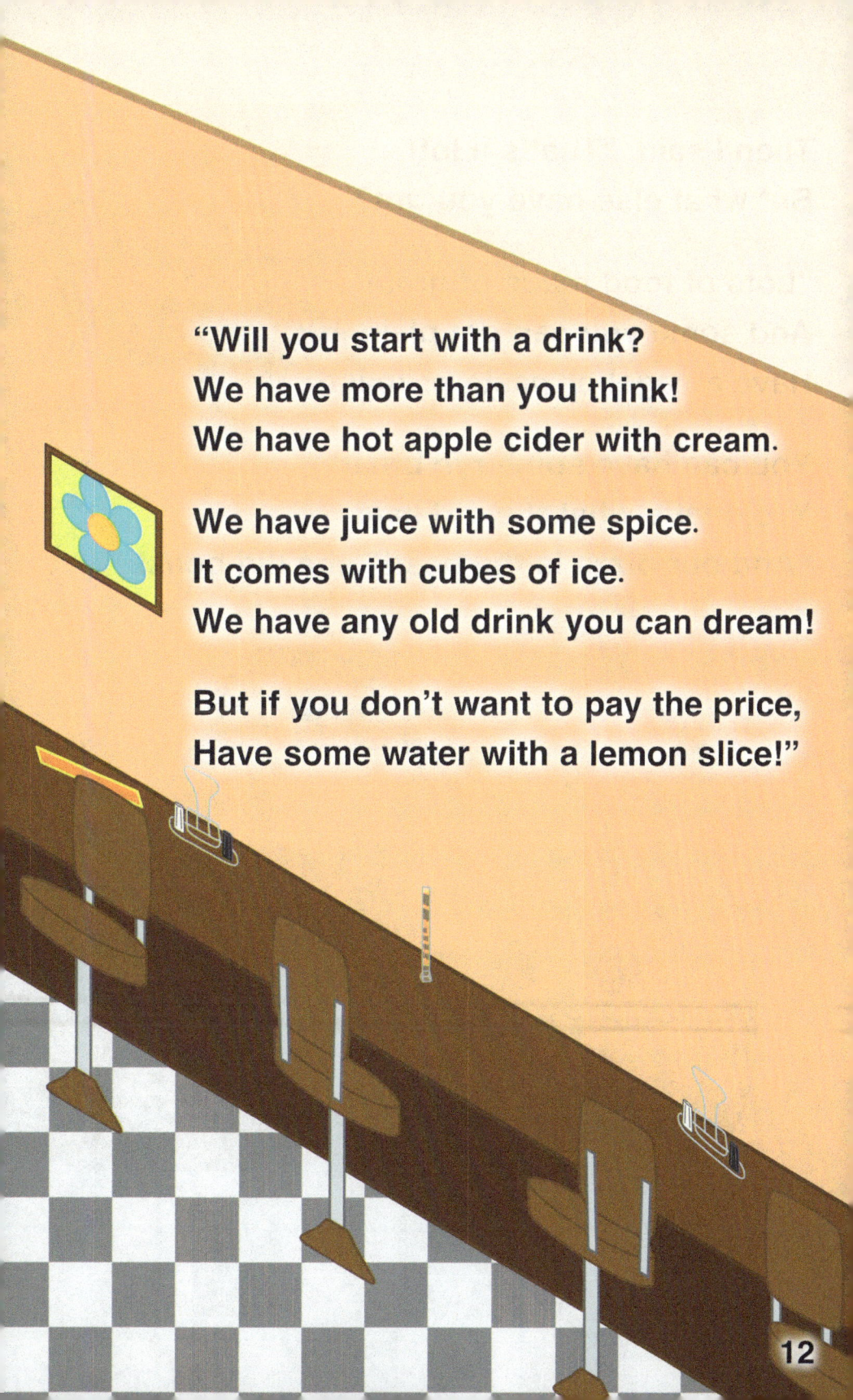

"Will you start with a drink?
We have more than you think!
We have hot apple cider with cream.

We have juice with some spice.
It comes with cubes of ice.
We have any old drink you can dream!

But if you don't want to pay the price,
Have some water with a lemon slice!"

Then I said, "That's a lot!
But what else have you got?"

"Lots of food made of grain
And some you can get plain.
Have a bagel or pasta or toast!

You can have some rye bread."
Yes, that's what the girl said.
"And our pizza is the best!" she did boast.

"Top your pizza with meat.
It's all made of whole wheat!
We can cut off the crust, if you want.

With your toast, have grape jelly
If you'd like for your belly.
In this diner, you can end your food hunt!"

And then I did say,
"Hold on now, okay?
I don't want your grain.
It's bad for my brain!

I'm no bird that feeds
On stuff made of seeds.
I need food more real
To make up my meal!"

16

As I sat near a booth,
She said, "Got a sweet tooth?

Then you're in for a treat!
We have sugar that's sweet,
Or add maple syrup to your dish.

We also have honey
If you've got the money.
We even have candy, if you wish."

"No, no, I don't want that!"
I said fast as I could.
"That would make me feel sick,
I'm quite sure that it would!"

"Okay, then, let's see,"
The girl said to me.

"We could steam you some meat.
Tell me, what *will* you eat?
It would come with fresh fruit on the side.

How about a bowl of soup?
Or some chips in bean goop?
Or else hot spicy food that's deep fried?

Yes, that food sure has zing!
Tell me, what *can* I bring?
In this place, you're the king!"
But I sat and did not say a thing.

21

"Come on, what would you like?
Tell me, and I'll have Mike
Cook it up for you on a big plate.
Hurry up or it's going to be late!"

Now I, Kit, was not so quick,
For I didn't know what to pick.
My mind went off on the music.
Was this all some kind of trick?

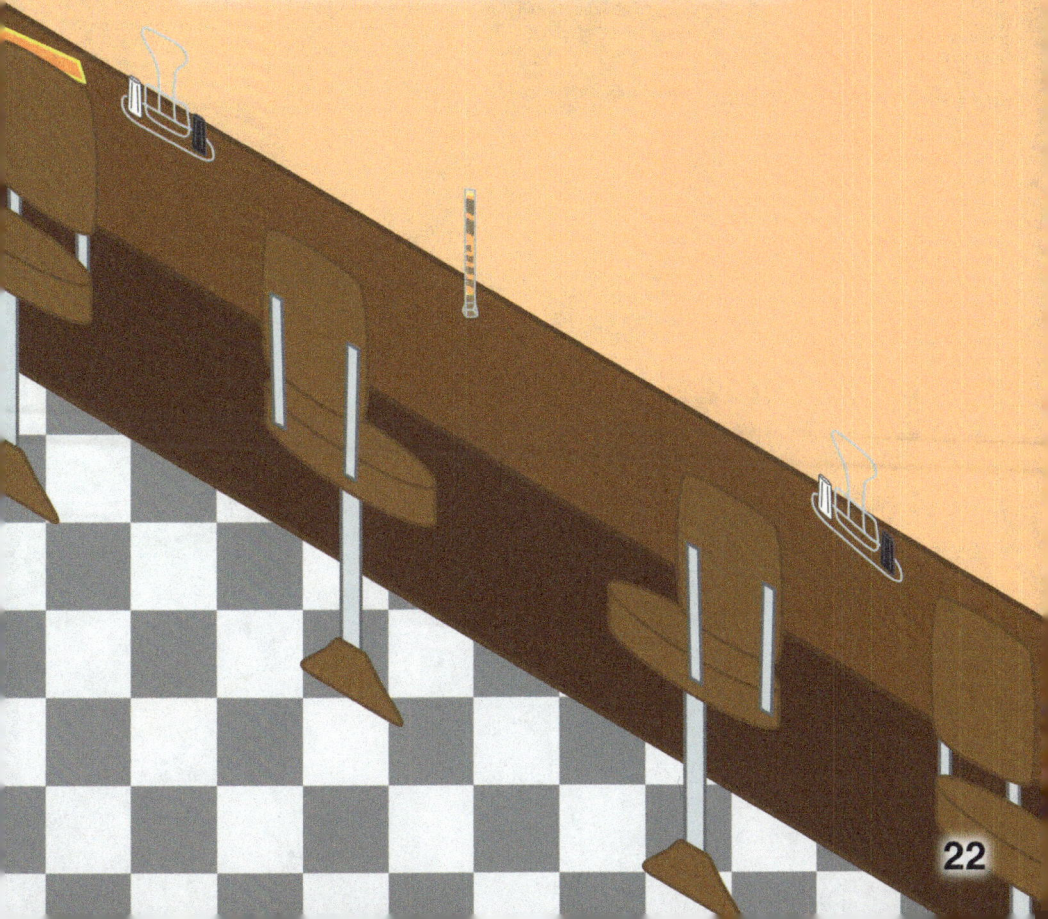

Now the girl did sound mad,
And no more was she glad!

Then she said with a shout,
"Hey now, look, what about
Our meal deal?
It sure has some value!"
Then, for real
She began to argue!

"Yeah, it comes with a drink
Plus a side of thick toast,
And I sure do think
That it's worth the most!

Now look, you don't have to feast.
Just order some food at least!"

"I'll just have to go
If you don't order soon.
Come on, don't be slow!
I will bring you a spoon
And a fork and a knife.
I can't stand here and wait
To get food on your plate
For the rest of my life!"

Now the woman did not look happy.
In fact, I think that she was angry.

So I took the clue
And set down the menu.

"I'll just have a salad."
Yes, that was what I said.
"With small bits of bacon.
Thank you, my dear Susan."

With eyes wide, she said, "Is that a joke?"
I said, "No, I want just what I spoke."

She did bring me my food,
And no more was she rude!

The food was so tasty
That my plate was soon empty!

Once I had eaten,
And I was all done,
When I was just then
Going out to have fun,
I began to walk out
So I could roam about.

I said, "Now that I've dined,
I think I would not mind
To come back here some time for a snack.

When I get in the mood
For a bit of good food,
I will think of this place and come back!"

She did not like my style
Or the curve of my lip,
But that woman did smile
When she saw the big tip!

Ah, yes, it is such a great day!
As I left, I could hear Susan say,

"Come back for your meals
Or when it just feels
Like you want a good snack to munch.

When you want a feast,
Or a salad at least,
I'll bring you what you'd like for lunch!"

Words in this book (new words are in **bold**):

1-letter words: a   I

2-letter words:

ah	by	if	my	or
an	do	in	no	so
as	go	is	of	to
at	I'd	it	oh	up
be	I'm	me	on	we

3-letter words:

add	did	how	off	tag
air	eat	I'll	old	the
all	end	I've	our	tip
and	for	**ice**	out	top
any	fun	it's	pay	two
bad	get	its	**rye**	was
big	got	Kit	sat	way
bit	had	lip	saw	wow
but	has	lot	say	yes
can	her	mad	see	you
cut	hey	not	set	
day	hot	now	she	

4-letter words:

also	best	bits	can't	come
back	bird	**bowl**	care	cook
bean	bite	came	clue	deal

4-letter words (continued):

dear	grew	made	rest	this
deep	hair	make	roam	time
dish	hand	meal	**rude**	took
does	have	meat	said	**tops**
don't	hear	**menu**	**sick**	true
done	**heed**	**Mike**	side	wait
down	here	mind	**slot**	walk
each	hold	mood	slow	want
else	hunt	more	sold	we've
even	item	most	some	well
eyes	**joke**	much	song	went
fact	just	name	soon	what
fast	kind	near	**soup**	when
feel	**king**	neat	such	wide
flat	know	need	sung	will
food	lady	nice	sure	wish
fork	late	okay	take	with
gain	left	once	tell	**wore**
girl	let's	over	test	yeah
glad	life	**pass**	than	you'd
gold	like	**pick**	that	your
good	look	plus	then	**zing**
goop	lots	real	they	

5-letter words:

about	**apple**	**aware**	**began**
along	**apron**	bacon	belly
angry	**argue**	bagel	**boast**

34

5-letter words (continued):

booth	**going**	quite	**syrup**
brain	**grain**	**salad**	**table**
bread	**grape**	**scent**	**tasty**
bring	**great**	**seeds**	**thank**
brown	happy	**shops**	**that's**
candy	**honey**	**shout**	there
chips	hurry	**slice**	**thick**
cider	**jelly**	small	thing
clear	**juice**	smell	think
comes	**kinds**	smile	**toast**
could	knife	**snack**	**tooth**
cream	least	**sound**	**treat**
crust	**lemon**	**speed**	**trick**
cubes	looks	spice	**tummy**
curve	lunch	**spicy**	twice
didn't	**maple**	**split**	**value**
dined	**meals**	**spoke**	**water**
diner	**money**	**spoon**	**wheat**
dream	**munch**	stand	**where**
drink	**music**	start	while
eaten	**order**	**steam**	**whole**
empty	**pasta**	still	woman
feast	**pizza**	**stood**	**worth**
feeds	place	stuff	**would**
feels	**plain**	**style**	**you'll**
fresh	**plate**	sugar	**you're**
fried	**price**	**Susan**	**you've**
fruit	quick	**sweet**	**yummy**

Kit Explores The Earth

An Easy-Start Reader
Level C, Book 3

by
Max Loony

Kit Beginning Reader Books

Level C: Kit Is Reading Now

Book C-3: Kit Explores The Earth

Written by Max Loony

Concepts in this book*:
- Written in past tense with simple sentences and rhyme schemes
- Only short words (1-5 letters)
- Short vowel sounds in various previous patterns
- Long vowel sounds in various previous patterns
- One-syllable short vowel sound in pattern —CCe
- Vowel combinations (*ie, oi*) in patterns —C*ie*C— and —C*oi*C—
- Vowel combination (*ou*) making three different sounds in pattern —C*ou*C—
- Strong "g" sound in consonant-vowel combo beginning *gu*—
- Strong "f" sound in consonant combo *ph*
- Several new two- and three-consonant blends (—dst, —fth, —nth, —rch, —rg—, —rld, —rst, spr—, str—, —tch, thr—, —wd, —xth)
- Many new two-syllable words including new patterns aCCVC, V*qu*VC, CVCCV, VCVVC, CCVCV, *qu*VVC, and CVVCy
- A new short contraction using 5 letters (*what's*)
- A new acronym (*UFO*)
- Several new phonetic exceptions (*again, ahead, earth, echo, heart, jewel, learn, ocean, soul, their, truth*)

*Word Pattern Key: C=Consonant, V=Vowel, *italics*=a specific letter, —(dash)=start or end of word

Download free parent/teacher guide at:
 readiculousbooks.com/kit

Copyright © 2023 Read-iculous Books

All rights reserved. Reproduction of this work, in whole or in part, in any manner whatsoever, is strictly prohibited, except for brief quotations embodied in critical articles and reviews.

BOOK C-3: KIT EXPLORES THE EARTH

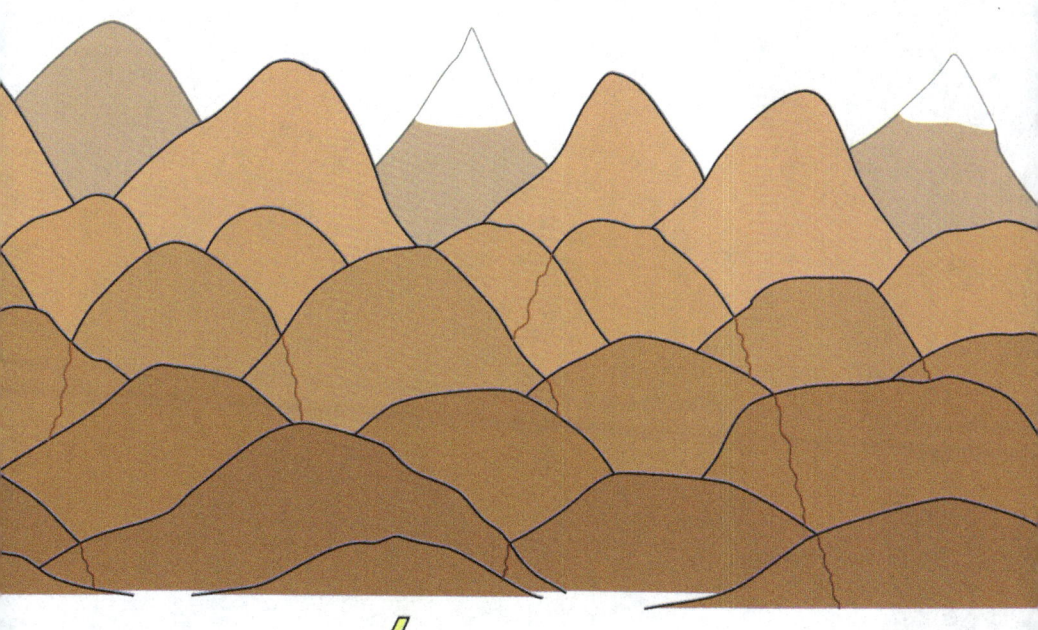

by Max Loony

When I first came to Earth,
I said, "What is this place?"
It was like a new birth
As I flew in from space.

This new world was so fine
And so blue and so round.
From below it did shine.
What is this I have found?

With the sky over my head
And the world under my feet,
With a big smile I said,
"Hey, this place sure looks neat!"

For what it is worth,
I saw that the sea fills
So much of the earth,
But the rest has some hills!

And then I said aloud,
"Now I am going down!"
I went into a cloud,
Then flew over a town!

I flew next to a plane.
I went near a long train.
It had cars in a chain.
That's a lot for my brain!

Now I went down so quick
That I fell like a brick!

After that, I flew west,
And I went past all that,
For I had a new quest:
Find a place that is flat!

When I came from the sky,
I went on down the coast.
It was low and not high,
And I like that the most!

Along the coast is the beach
Where the ocean meets the land.
Then a nice spot I did reach,
And what's all over it? Sand!

As down the beach I flew,
I said, "Wow! What a view!"

There were boats out in the sea,
And waves along the shore,
And so much water to see
That I'd never seen more!

Of my stops, this is first!
And it's sure not the worst!
Then I found a good place to park.
I got out for a shell.
I said, "Hey, this one's swell!
Now it seems I have left my mark.
To stay here would be handy,
But this place is too sandy!
And I say, could that be a shark?"

I would not stay that day,
So I went on my way.

I flew over some trees—
Yes, a creek and a wood—
And I said, "What are these?
This looks great, this looks good!"

Then I came to a brook,
And I took a close look.
It ran into a river,
And I said, "This is super!"

The river from above
Looks just like a big crack,
And I can't help but love
That it's blue and not black!

As my ship I did steer,
Very fast was my pace!
I'm so glad that I'm here,
And not out in deep space!

I saw so very much
That I would like to touch.
It gave me so many ideas!

In my ship I can sneak,
So I took a quick peek,
And I came to know many areas!

The third place I did visit
Made my soul full of glee!
Does this world have no limit?
Now my stops count to three.

What is all of this here?
And where do I begin?
In this spot that is clear,
I could see a cabin.

Some steps led to a porch
That was lit with a torch.

Two guys sat up there—
Each one in a chair.

They had set down their packs
To kick back and relax.

12

By a large patch of grass
Hung a bell made of brass.
Next to that were some tents
Where the woods are so dense.

13

Then I saw lots of smoke!
What was that all about?
I did not want to choke,
So I did not get out!

By the fire of their camp,
Here is what I did learn:
There was a shirt that was damp,
And it was hung with a clamp
Far away so that it would not burn!

Next I came to a city
While the sun was still shiny.

Look at this busy scene!
Do you see what I mean?

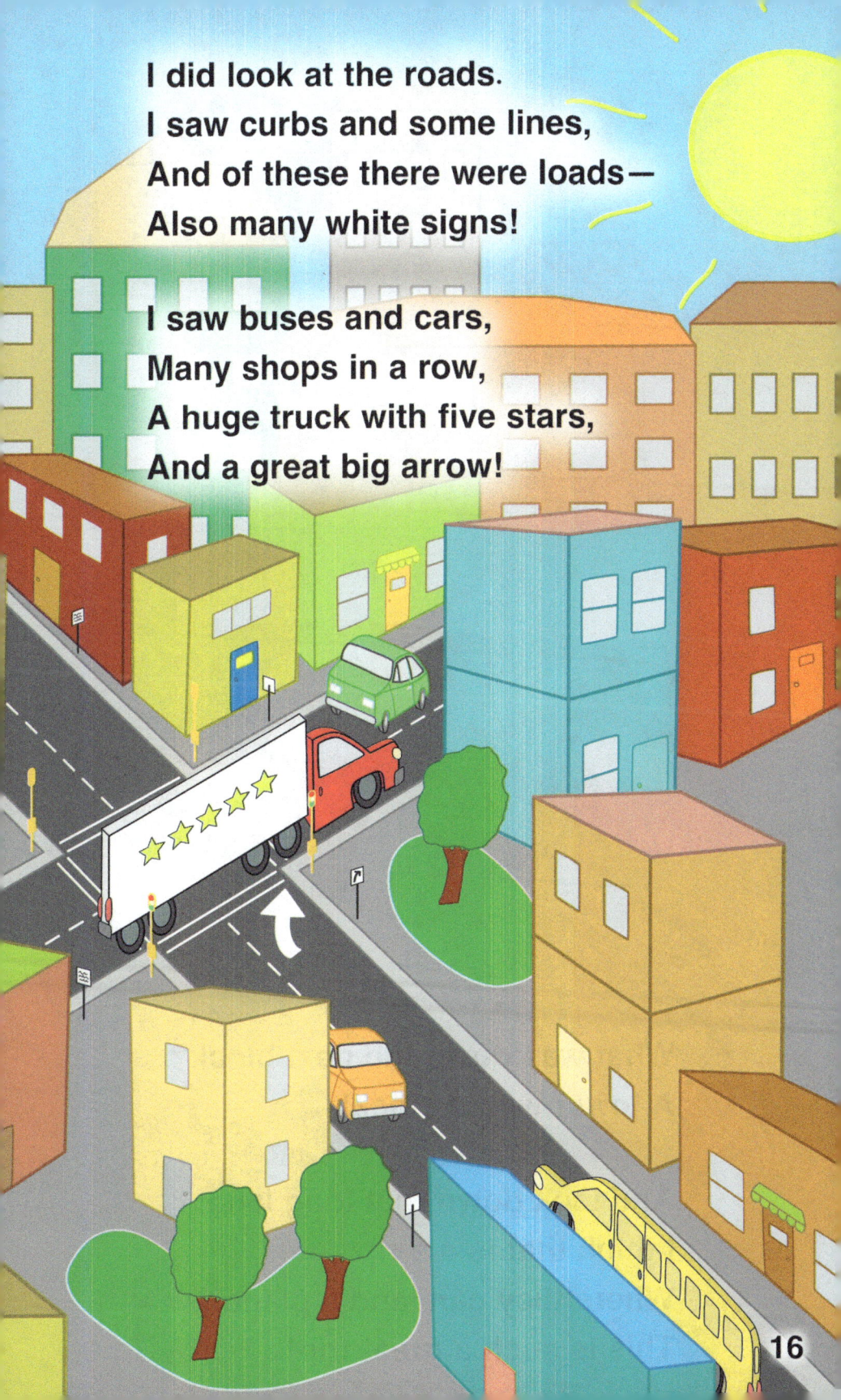

I did look at the roads.
I saw curbs and some lines,
And of these there were loads—
Also many white signs!

I saw buses and cars,
Many shops in a row,
A huge truck with five stars,
And a great big arrow!

What was down the next block?
A tower with a clock!

And look down that long lane!
I think that is a strip
Where they can land a plane.
This is such a great trip!

And then I was aware
Of a group of some kind.
Some of them had long hair
That was stuck in a bind!

It was risky and scary.
They were noisy and hairy.

So I did not land there
In the midst of the crowd.
I could see dirty air.
It was also too loud!

18

Then I went to a mount.
It had lots of small hills.
How many can I count?
They were like great big pills!
Maybe fifty or forty?
Each would make a good story!

Far away they had snow.
In the sun, it did glow.
Some of the hills came to a point!

Side by side the hills press.
It's a big but nice mess,
And there is a crack at each joint.

Look at all of those lines!
On the hills each crack did pave
A path where water had run.

What if these hills have mines?
I said, "If I find a cave,
I think that it would be fun!"

Then I saw a small sign
With a board and a nail
At the start of a trail
To a cave or a mine!

Now this was my fifth stop,
So I hit the brake and did drop.

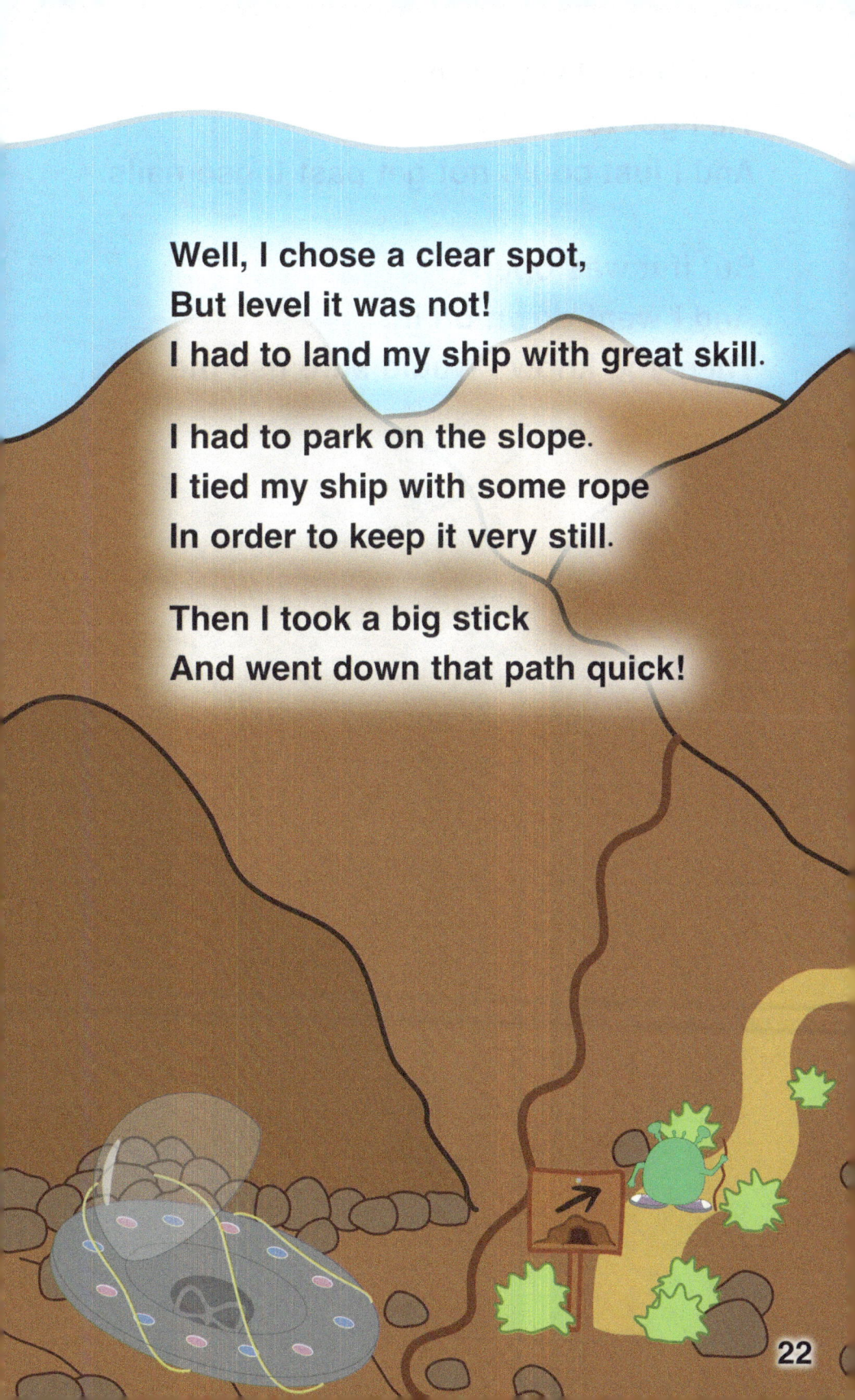

Well, I chose a clear spot,
But level it was not!
I had to land my ship with great skill.

I had to park on the slope.
I tied my ship with some rope
In order to keep it very still.

Then I took a big stick
And went down that path quick!

I did think I was brave
Till I got to the cave,
And I just could not get past those nails.

But if it was open
And I went down on in,
Then you know I would sure use the rails!

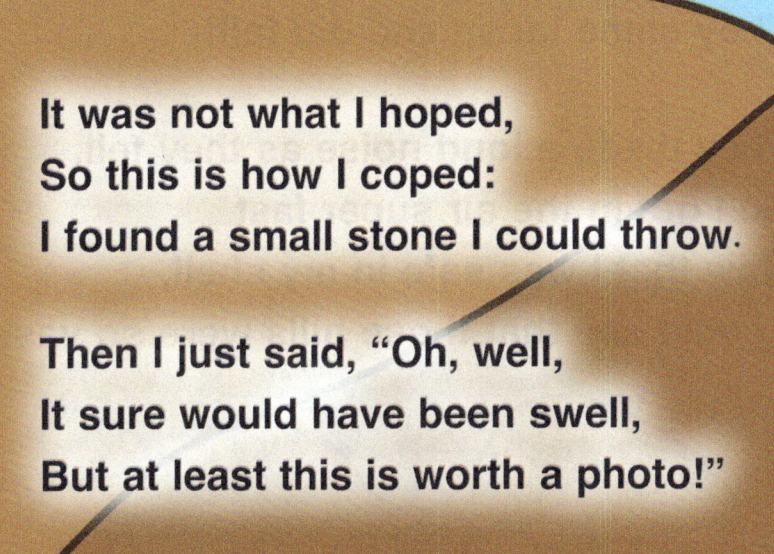

It was not what I hoped,
So this is how I coped:
I found a small stone I could throw.

Then I just said, "Oh, well,
It sure would have been swell,
But at least this is worth a photo!"

I took the rope off my ship.
Then it began to slip!
Over the rocks I did crawl.
They came loose and did fall!

They made a loud noise as they fell,
So I got in the air super fast.
Now that I was safe in my shell,
I could see that those hills were so vast!

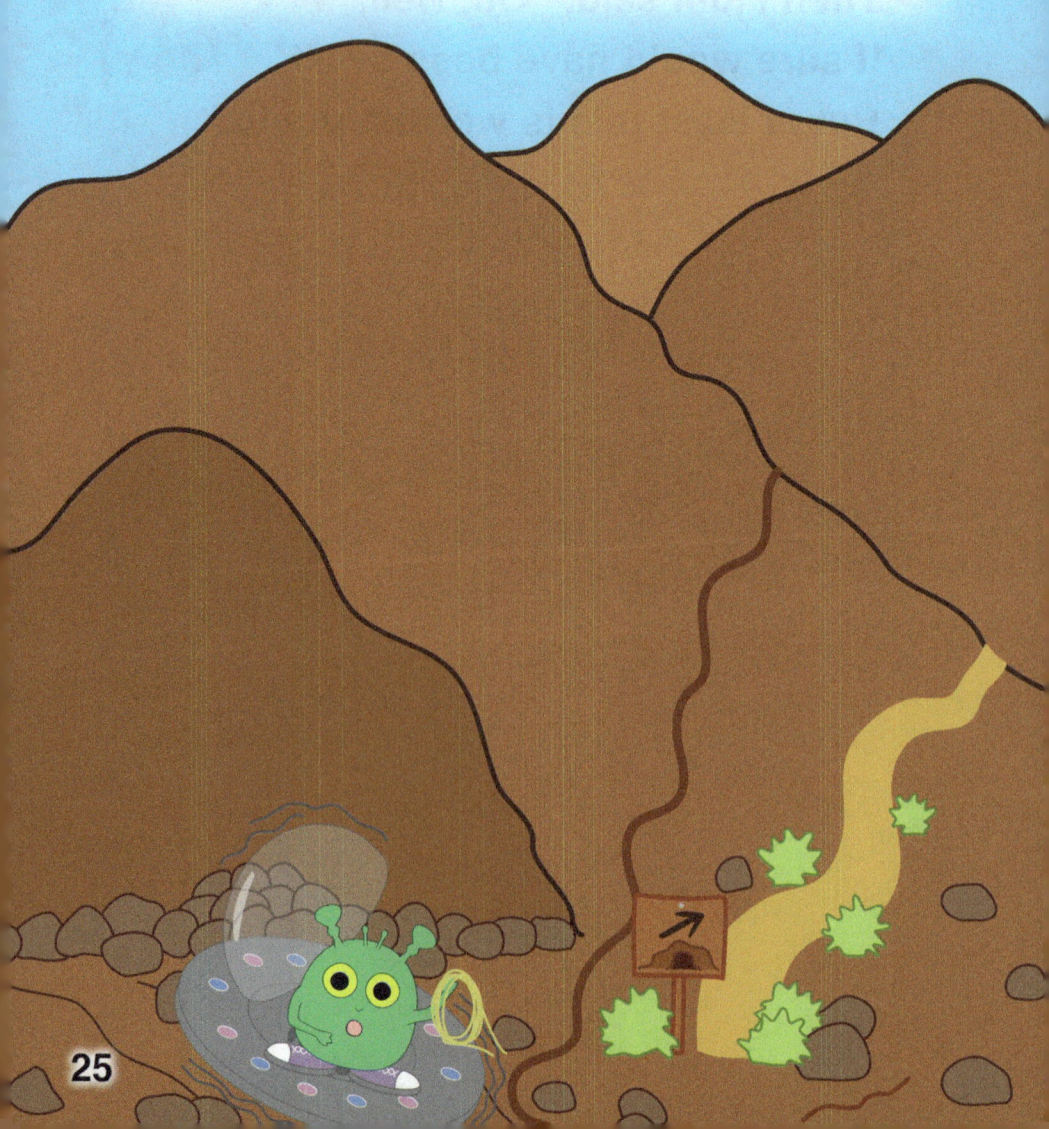

Rocks came down in a spray
As I flew off the cliff.
Then, I went to see more of the hills.

Well, I did this all day
Until I was quite stiff.
See, I don't have to work or pay bills!

Now my ship had good lift,
And my speed was so swift,
That soon I began to get dizzy!

I knew what I was doing,
But not where I was going.
Now you may think I am a bit crazy!

The sixth spot I did see
Just made my heart soar!
It sure did click with me!
How could there be more?

I flew over green parks,
Then I saw an old mound
Which had lots of odd marks.
I said, "Look what I found!
And its shape is so round!"

Way down far below
I knew I must go
And see what is under this cloud.

When I got close to it,
I just had to admit,
That then in a flash I felt proud!

28

I found a good place to land
And park my ship on the green.
This place did not look bland.
I said, "What a great scene!

Yes, I like being here
And how it makes me feel!
It's a field that is clear
With great rocks in a wheel!"

Very soon, there I stood,
And it sure felt quite good!
Yes, the air was so thick,
I could feel the magic!

Front and back and both sides there was stone,
As I stood in the grass and the dust.
I did stand on that spot all alone,
While the winds came and went in a gust!

They blew in a nice fog
Like you'd see in a bog.

In the mist I did blink,
For this place made me think.
I could feel such a deep, deep peace.
Here the noise of the world did cease!

It was quiet and cool.
Yes, this place was a jewel!
Now my soul was so full!
I don't know its equal!

Such big rocks in a ring!
Each stone stood on its end!
I felt like I could sing,
And my voice would just blend
With the songs of those long, long ago.
In my mind, I could hear the echo!

Then after I had sung,
I began to feel young!
In this place is a truth
I did seek in my youth!

"I would stay here for weeks
Or a month—maybe two!
It is what my soul seeks."
I could feel that was true.

The sun set as it shone
Onto each great big stone!
Wait—what was that odd tone?
Next I found that I was not alone!

Past the rocks ran some guys
With their hands in the air.
Very wide were their eyes,
And I, Kit, they did scare!

Were these guys upset?
For they broke the quiet!
They said, "Look, it's a UFO!"

Now I, Kit, did not know
What on earth that could be.
I did not wait to see,
So I said, "I guess I'll just go!
I'll get in and boost the turbo!"

37

I got in my ship quick!
With my hand I did flick,
Then I was way up high in the air!

They did point to the sky,
And I did not know why.
You see, I was too shy
To stay down and wait for them there.

Now I, Kit, am not truly upset,
For I'd say it was a nice visit.
They say that the sky is the limit.
Not for me! I'll fly past this comet!

This world I came to see,
I think you would agree,
It's like a dream come true!
From up here it is such a nice view!

As I left that new place
And I went into space,
Here is what I had said:
"I don't know what's ahead,
And I do not know when,
But I'm sure I'll come back here again!"

Words in this book (new words are in **bold**):

1-letter words: a   I

2-letter words:

am	by	if	my	or
an	do	in	no	so
as	go	is	of	to
at	I'd	it	oh	up
be	I'm	me	on	

3-letter words:

ago	fly	Kit	pay	too
air	fog	**led**	ran	two
all	for	**lit**	row	**UFO**
and	fun	lot	run	use
are	get	low	sat	was
big	got	may	saw	way
bit	had	new	say	why
bog	has	not	sea	wow
but	hey	now	see	yes
can	hit	odd	set	you
day	how	off	shy	
did	I'll	old	sky	
end	it's	one	sun	
far	its	out	the	

4-letter words:

| also | back | **bell** | blew | both |
| away | been | **bind** | blue | **burn** |

41

4-letter words (continued):

busy	from	like	path	this
came	full	long	**pave**	tied
camp	gave	look	peek	till
can't	glad	lots	rest	**tone**
cars	glee	loud	ring	took
cave	glow	love	**rope**	town
city	good	made	safe	trip
come	gust	make	said	true
cool	guys	many	sand	**vast**
damp	hair	**mark**	**seek**	very
deep	hand	mean	seen	**view**
does	have	mess	ship	wait
don't	head	mind	side	want
down	hear	mine	sign	well
drop	help	**mist**	sing	went
dust	here	more	slip	were
each	high	most	snow	**west**
echo	hill	much	soar	what
eyes	huge	must	some	when
fall	hung	**nail**	soon	wide
fast	into	near	**soul**	with
feel	just	neat	spot	wood
feet	keep	next	stay	work
fell	kick	nice	stop	you'd
felt	kind	one's	such	
find	knew	onto	sung	
fine	know	open	sure	
fire	land	over	that	
five	lane	pace	them	
flat	left	park	then	
flew	**lift**	past	they	

42

5-letter words:

about	**brave**	**dizzy**	**learn**
above	**brick**	**doing**	least
admit	**broke**	dream	**level**
after	**brook**	**earth**	**limit**
again	**buses**	**equal**	**lines**
agree	**cabin**	**field**	loads
ahead	**cease**	**fifth**	looks
alone	**chain**	**fifty**	**loose**
along	**chair**	**fills**	**magic**
aloud	**choke**	**first**	makes
areas	**chose**	**flash**	**marks**
arrow	**clamp**	**flick**	**maybe**
aware	clear	**forty**	**meets**
beach	click	**found**	**midst**
began	**cliff**	front	**mines**
begin	clock	going	**month**
being	close	grass	**mound**
below	**cloud**	great	**mount**
bills	**coast**	green	**nails**
birth	**comet**	**group**	**never**
black	**coped**	**guess**	**noise**
bland	could	**hairy**	**noisy**
blend	**count**	hands	**ocean**
blink	**crack**	**handy**	order
block	**crawl**	**heart**	**packs**
board	**crazy**	**hills**	**parks**
boats	**creek**	**hoped**	**patch**
boost	**crowd**	**ideas**	**peace**
brain	**curbs**	**jewel**	**photo**
brake	**dense**	**joint**	**pills**
brass	**dirty**	**large**	place

5-letter words (continued):

plane	**shiny**	stood	**truth**
point	**shirt**	**stops**	**turbo**
porch	**shone**	**story**	**under**
press	shops	**strip**	**until**
proud	**shore**	stuck	**upset**
quest	**sides**	**super**	**visit**
quick	**signs**	swell	**voice**
quiet	**sixth**	**swift**	water
quite	**skill**	**tents**	**waves**
rails	**slope**	that's	weeks
reach	small	**their**	**what's**
relax	smile	there	**wheel**
risky	**smoke**	these	where
river	**sneak**	thick	**which**
roads	**songs**	think	while
rocks	space	**third**	white
round	speed	those	**winds**
sandy	**spray**	**three**	**woods**
scare	stand	**throw**	**world**
scary	stars	**torch**	**worst**
scene	start	**touch**	worth
seeks	**steer**	**tower**	would
seems	**steps**	**trail**	**young**
shape	stick	**train**	**youth**
shark	**stiff**	trees	
shell	still	truck	
shine	stone	**truly**	

Kit Loves Life!

An Easy-Start Reader
Level C, Book 4

by
Max Loohy

READ-ICULOUS BOOKS

Kit Beginning Reader Books

Level C: Kit Is Reading Now

Book C-4: Kit Loves Life!

Written by Max Loony

Concepts in this book*:
- Longer sentences with more complex rhyme schemes
- Only short words (1-5 letters)
- Short vowel sounds in various previous patterns
- Long vowel sounds in various previous patterns
- One-syllable long vowel sound in pattern —*ste*
- Single vowel (*i*), making long "i" vowel sound, in pattern CC*i*CC
- Vowel-consonant ending exception sound (—*ght*) with silent *gh*
- Silent "h" in consonant combo beginnings *gh*— and *rh*—
- A few new two- and three-consonant blends (—*bt*, *gh*—, *rh*—, *squ*—)
- Many new two-syllable words including new patterns VCVCC, CVVCC, VVCC*y*, and CVCV*y*
- A couple new three-syllable words in new pattern VCVC*y* (*enemy, every*)
- A couple new short contractions using 5 letters (*aren't, here's*)
- Introduction to use of semicolon (;)
- Introduction to possessive words with apostrophes using 5 letters
- Several new phonetic exceptions (*choir, early, fours, heard, lose, moves, reply, shoes, tired, veins, weird, wound, yours*)

*Word Pattern Key: C=Consonant, V=Vowel, *italics*=a specific letter, —(dash)=start or end of word

Download free parent/teacher guide at:
    readiculousbooks.com/kit

Copyright © 2023 Read-iculous Books

All rights reserved. Reproduction of this work, in whole or in part, in any manner whatsoever, is strictly prohibited, except for brief quotations embodied in critical articles and reviews.

BOOK C-4: KIT LOVES LIFE!

by Max Loony

I knew it was early
When I woke to the sun.
My hair was not curly,
For, you see, I have none!

Now I rub both my eyes
And I open them wide,
Then with joy I arise
From my sleep on my side.

Next, my head I will shake
Till I'm fully awake!

I arose from my bed,
And I threw off the sheet.
I did think in my head
That today will be sweet!

"Why would you think that?" You may say.
Just wait, let me tell you a story.
No, no, it will not take all day.
It's quite short, okay? So don't worry!

Now I'll teach you a thing
That I think you must know,
For in my soul it does burn.

So to you I'll now bring
From a long time ago
This thing that I had to learn:

The first thing that I do
Is my soul says, "Thank you
For the good, happy life that is mine!"

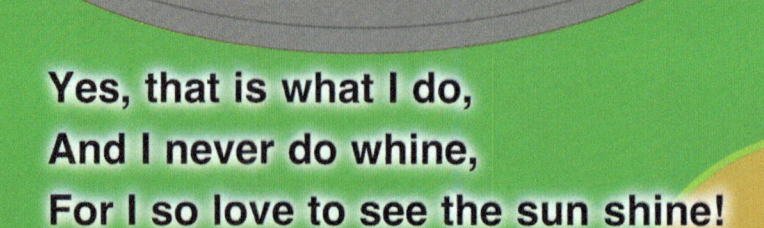

Yes, that is what I do,
And I never do whine,
For I so love to see the sun shine!

I'm so glad I have sight.
To be happy feels right.
I just love all the stuff that I see!

I'm alert and aware
As I sit in my chair,
And I also love that I am free!

Once I have a good grip
On the day,
I climb out of my ship
And I say,
"Now I'm fully alert!
I'll put my feet in the dirt,
For I truly like it that way!"
Oh yes, life is so great,
And I feel I can't wait
To begin on this fresh new day!

I don't care what I'm doing,
For I just love *being!*

Then I said with a smile.
"I'll have fun for a while!"

You may think I am silly
And I have a big belly,
But you know I can make a good rhyme.

I'm not a bit bossy
And I do not get angry.
Well, at least that's true most of the time!

For I, Kit, have deep peace in my mind.
Yes, I'm Kit and I'm ever so kind!

Now, when many see me,
They say, "He is cute as can be!
Just look at those shoes and that smile!"
And that's when I stay for a while.
But some don't want me there,
I say, "Okay, that's fair,"
For I'm still at peace in my soul,
And I won't lose track of my goal!

When I'm in a crowd,
I hear some say out loud,
"He's funny and dopey
And look at how happy!"
"But he's odd," some have said.
I'm not human—but I am a biped!

"What is that?" You want to know.
It's about how I go!
It just means that I walk on two feet.
Now you know that, so isn't that neat?

biped=2 feet

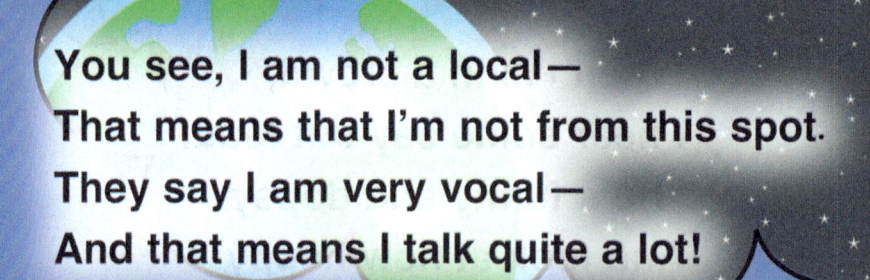

You see, I am not a local—
That means that I'm not from this spot.
They say I am very vocal—
And that means I talk quite a lot!

While I might be an odd one,
I still like to just have fun,
"Odd" is only a label,
And I know that I'm able
To let it roll off of my back!
I don't care and I do not keep track!

To such words I reply,
With a gleam in my eye,
"I like who I am,
And that's not a sham!
I am never fake
In the morn when I wake,
For I think life is great every day!
It's so fun, and I like it that way!"

You may think that I'm lucky
And that's why I'm so happy,
But that is not how it goes.
Stay alert, here's the truth:
When I was but a youth,
In my mind, to be happy I chose.

I'm alive and I love it!
And I do not covet
Any items that I do not own.

I love life for it does
Help me learn new ideas—
Lots of new stuff that I had not known.

I love a party or game—
Or to play a fun sport.
I won't feel any shame
In spite of the fact that I'm short!

Dan Sam Sue Pam ? ?

It's not all fun and games,
For at times there are names
I can't think of—and that bugs my brain!
But I won't let that be a drain!

I'll move right along,
And I won't miss a beat.
I might sing a song
Or else dance with my feet!

When I feel all alone
Or I get a bit bored,
Then I say, "Hey, I'll just sit and think!"

I'll put away my phone
And I'll plug in its cord,
Then I'll write stuff with blue and black ink!

Or else that's when Kit cooks
Or sits and takes looks
At what's in a few good books!

It's not that I never make an error.
It's just that I learn from stuff I do wrong.
And if I have to do some hard labor,
I'll get that work done while I hum a song!

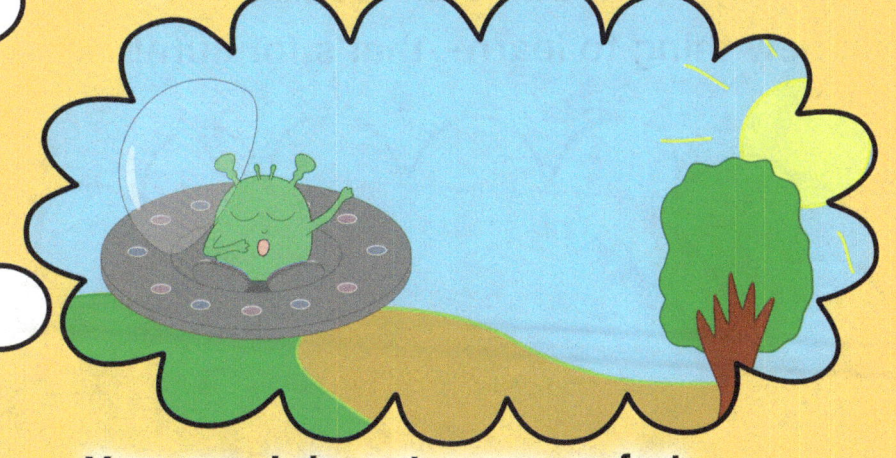

You see, I do not worry or fret,
For every day since I was born,
It's never the same in the morn!
So why would I worry about it?
I don't do it, for it's a bad habit!
Life is good, and I never doubt it!

If I feel awful
Or life is not usual,
If I have the blues
Or play a game and lose,
If I don't feel brave
Or lack food that I crave,
If there is some issue
Or my buddy does argue,

I can still stay quite calm, that is true.
And guess what? You could stay calm, too!

For in any event that can occur
Is a new thing to learn—that's for sure!

When I'm stiff or sore
Or I have a hard chore,
If I'm tired or in pain
Or my shoes have a stain,
Or if I've got a wound or a fever,
I will do no harm
And I'll keep my charm—
Plus I have my good sense of humor!

Each and every day is a new one,
And each day I look for new ways to have fun!

See, I chose to be happy
Even when I feel badly,
For real joy comes from the heart!
You can do it, too—yes, you can start!

If you can hear me, I just have to state:
All the stuff I can do with this body is great!

I can touch with my hands.
I can eat with my mouth.
I can walk to new lands.
I can point north and south!

mouth →

← hands →

17

I love my cool shoes;
Them I'll never lose!
I can spin on my heels.
Yes, I know how that feels!

My shoes have such style!
They sure make me smile,
And my smile is so wide
That each cheek moves aside!

cheek cheek
smile
shoes

My whole body is green,
But my teeth are so white.
Ask me why they aren't seen:
I keep them out of sight!

My brain is not dumb,
For I am so smart.
In my chest, like a drum,
Goes the beat of my heart.
On each hand is a thumb;
With them, I can make art!

In my veins, I have blood,
But it's not red like yours!
When I play in the mud,
I get down on all fours!
I would float in a flood,
And I would not need oars!

As if it were a sport,
With my arms I would swim.
But my legs are so short,
You can't even see them!

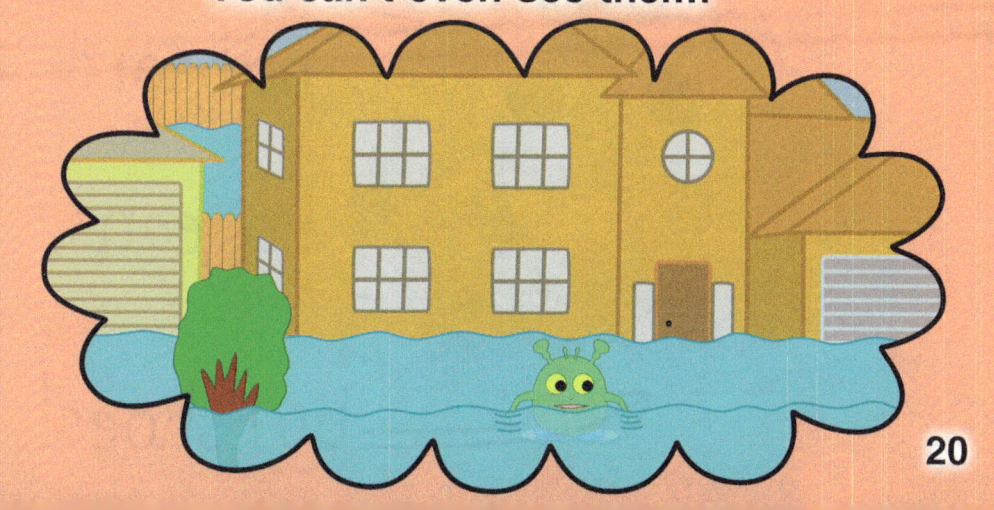

Now, I don't need a brush
Or some jeans or a dress.
I won't be in a rush
With my hair in a mess!

You see, I have no beard
And no braid and no hair.
You may think that is weird,
But I truly don't care!
And I still love the shoes that I wear!

no braid
no beard
no jeans
but shoes!

Yes, my image is fine
And so is my spine,
For it goes up my back in a line.

spine
back

belly/chest

At a party I'd dance,
If I were a guest,
Until all of them knew my name!

I don't even wear pants.
See my belly and chest?
Take a look! They are one and the same!

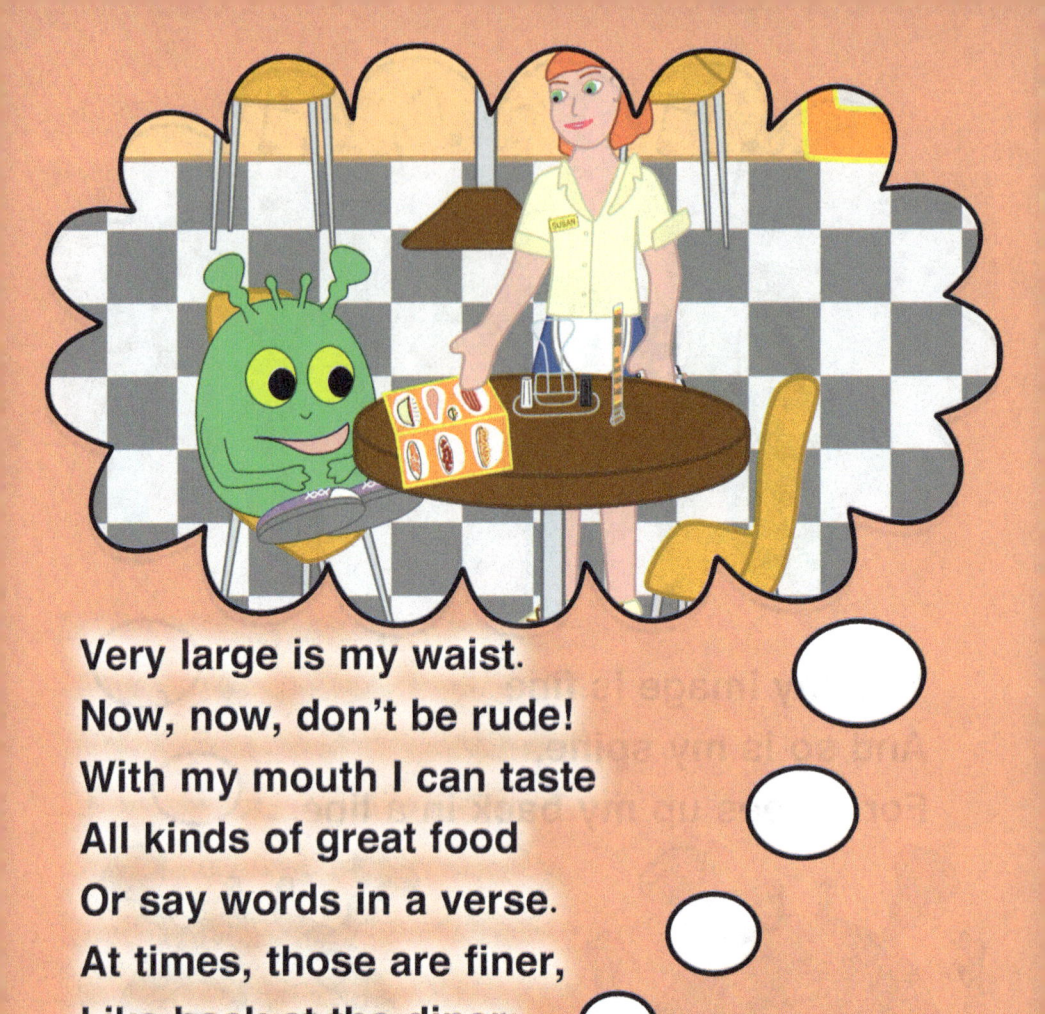

Very large is my waist.
Now, now, don't be rude!
With my mouth I can taste
All kinds of great food
Or say words in a verse.
At times, those are finer,
Like back at the diner;
Other times, they are quite a bit worse!

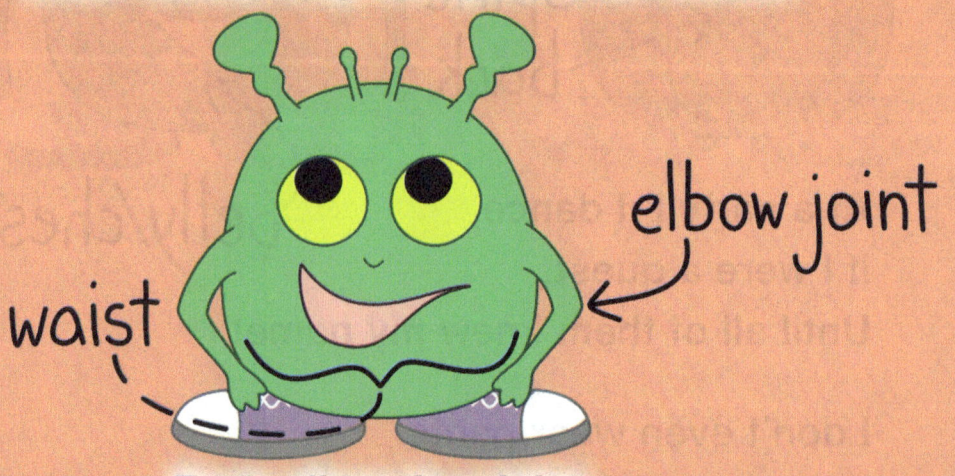

elbow joint

waist

Each elbow is a joint.
Now have I made my point?

I take care of my body with pride,
And I keep my shoes neat on each side!

From the front to the rear,
Yeah, I could make a list.
All my parts are right here,
And each hand has a wrist—
One on the left and one on the right.
Yeah, I could make a fist
If I got in a fight,
And I could punch with all of my might!

But to turn the other cheek
Would not say I am weak.
It says that I have no enemy.
It's that I'm good and happy and free!

What did I put on when I awoke?
Not armor nor a robe nor a cloak.
I've just got socks and shoes:
That's the stuff that I use!
Yes, I tell you the truth, not a joke!

When I went to that store
And I got that red suit,
Some would stare and adore.
Many said, "That looks cute!"

But I don't wear it much—
No, not even a shirt—
For it takes work and such,
And it drags in the dirt!

If it made me trip
And I lost my grip,
Well then, I might get hurt!

No, I don't look human,
But I'm still lots of fun!

I don't have sharp claws
Or four furry paws
Or a beak or some fangs or a tail.

I don't look like a puppy,
And I'm sure not a bunny!
I am not like a snake or a whale.

I am not beast or bird—
They don't utter a word!
By now I'm sure you've heard
All the talk that I've given,
For I'm just a funny green alien!

28

In your world, I'm a guest—
And one with lots of zest!

But in my own world, when I'm back at home,
Want to know what I do when I do not roam?

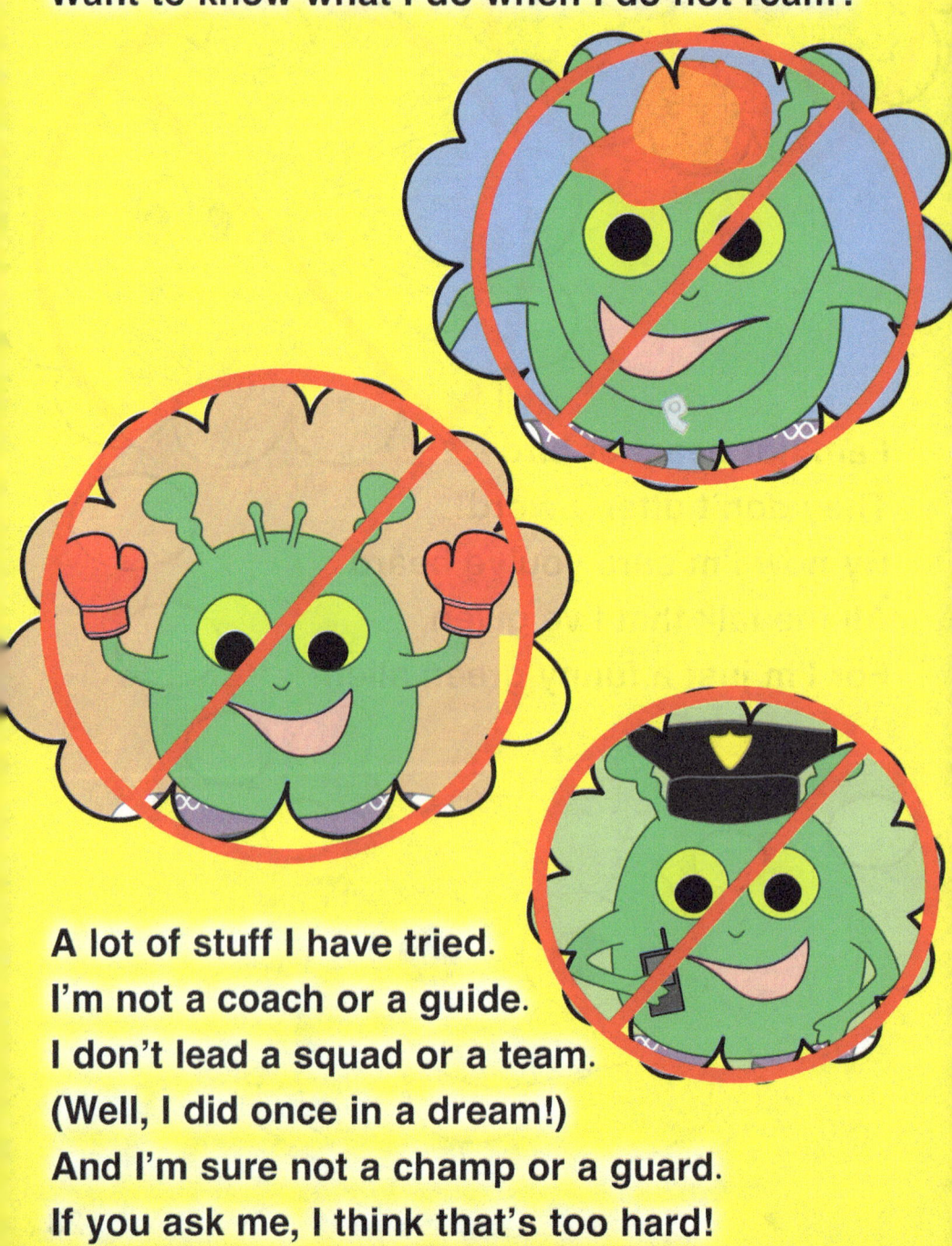

A lot of stuff I have tried.
I'm not a coach or a guide.
I don't lead a squad or a team.
(Well, I did once in a dream!)
And I'm sure not a champ or a guard.
If you ask me, I think that's too hard!

I'm not an angel or fairy.
I'm not a witch or a ghost.
You know that I'm not scary.
I'm just a small guy who loves life the most!

I'm not an actor or agent.
Now, it's not that I can't,
But I don't slay a giant
Or save the whole land!
I don't sing in the choir
Or play in the band!
But I'll sit by a fire
And write with my hand!

I do not fight crime.
I just don't have the time!
I don't catch the crook
Or get back what one stole.
I will sit with a book:
That's more like my goal!

I'm not a king or queen,
For I'm plain and I'm green.
Do you see what I mean?

I do not wear a crown
Or some long fancy gown,
For I'm not the chief or a ruler.

I don't stand very tall.
No one comes when I call.
But I dare say that I'm a bit cuter!

I may not be a ruler;
That is not what I do!
But I am a great tutor
Of a child, maybe two.

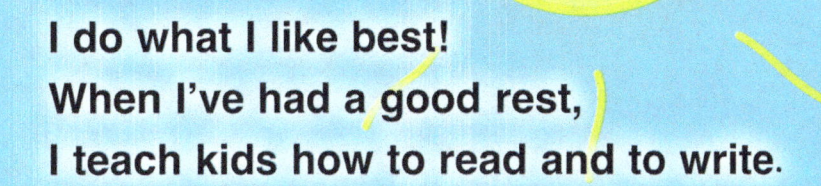

I do what I like best!
When I've had a good rest,
I teach kids how to read and to write.

What I love is what I do,
And I think you could, too,
For that is the thing that feels right!

I'm just happy being me!
That's the way I feel free!

Oh, I'm also a rider
And quite a proud owner
Of my very own ship,
And that's how I came on this trip!

Yes, my ship's super cool.
It is such a great tool!
I can zoom fast all over the place!

While it won't make a sound,
I can fly round and round
Or deep into the abyss of space!

Bye!

Words in this book (new words are in **bold**):

1-letter words: a　　I

2-letter words:

am	by	I'm	me	on
an	do	if	my	or
as	go	in	no	so
at	he	is	of	to
be	I'd	it	oh	up

3-letter words:

ago	day	hey	new	sit
all	did	how	**nor**	sun
and	eat	**hum**	not	the
any	eye	I'll	now	too
are	few	I've	odd	two
art	fly	ink	off	use
ask	for	it's	one	was
bad	fun	its	out	way
bed	get	joy	own	who
big	got	Kit	put	why
bit	guy	let	red	yes
but	had	lot	rub	you
bye	has	may	say	
can	he's	mud	see	

4-letter words:

| able | arms | back | beak | best |
| also | away | **band** | beat | bird |

37

4-letter words (continued):

blue	fake	isn't	mine	rude
body	fast	joke	miss	**rush**
book	feel	just	more	said
born	feet	keep	morn	same
both	fine	kids	most	save
bugs	fire	kind	move	says
burn	fist	king	much	seen
call	food	knew	must	**sham**
calm	four	know	name	ship
came	free	lack	neat	side
can't	**fret**	land	need	sing
care	from	lead	next	sits
cool	game	left	none	**slay**
cord	glad	legs	**oars**	some
cute	goal	life	okay	song
dare	goes	like	once	sore
deep	good	line	only	soul
dirt	**gown**	list	open	**spin**
does	grip	long	over	spot
don't	hair	look	pain	stay
done	hand	**lose**	paws	such
down	hard	lost	play	suit
drum	**harm**	lots	**plug**	sure
dumb	have	loud	plus	swim
each	head	love	read	tail
else	hear	made	real	take
even	help	make	rear	talk
ever	here	many	rest	tall
eyes	home	mean	roam	**team**
fact	hurt	mess	robe	tell
fair	into	mind	roll	that

4-letter words (continued):

them	trip	want	what	word
then	true	**ways**	when	work
they	turn	weak	wide	yeah
this	very	wear	will	your
till	wait	well	with	**zest**
time	wake	went	woke	zoom
tool	walk	were	won't	

5-letter words:

about	**badly**	**champ**	**curly**
abyss	**beard**	charm	**cuter**
actor	**beast**	**cheek**	**dance**
adore	begin	**chest**	diner
agent	being	**chief**	doing
alert	belly	**child**	**dopey**
alien	**biped**	**choir**	**doubt**
alive	black	chore	**drags**
alone	**blood**	chose	**drain**
along	**blues**	**claws**	dream
angel	books	**climb**	**dress**
angry	**bored**	**cloak**	**early**
aren't	**bossy**	**coach**	**elbow**
argue	**braid**	comes	**enemy**
arise	brain	**cooks**	**error**
armor	brave	could	**event**
arose	bring	**covet**	**every**
aside	**brush**	**crave**	**fairy**
awake	**buddy**	**crime**	**fancy**
aware	**bunny**	**crook**	**fangs**
awful	**catch**	crowd	feels
awoke	chair	**crown**	fever

5-letter words (continued):

fight	ideas	**party**	since
finer	**image**	peace	**sleep**
first	**issue**	**phone**	small
float	**items**	place	smart
flood	**jeans**	plain	smile
fours	joint	point	**snake**
fresh	kinds	**pride**	**socks**
front	**known**	proud	sound
fully	**label**	**punch**	**south**
funny	**labor**	**puppy**	space
furry	lands	**queen**	**spine**
games	large	quite	**spite**
ghost	learn	**reply**	**sport**
giant	least	**rhyme**	**squad**
given	**local**	**rider**	**stain**
gleam	looks	**right**	stand
great	**loves**	round	**stare**
green	**lucky**	**ruler**	start
guard	maybe	scary	**state**
guess	**means**	sense	stiff
guest	**might**	**shake**	still
guide	**mouth**	**shame**	**stole**
habit	**moves**	**sharp**	**store**
hands	**names**	**sheet**	story
happy	never	shine	stuff
heard	**north**	**ship's**	style
heart	**occur**	shirt	**super**
heels	**other**	**shoes**	sweet
here's	**owner**	short	**takes**
human	**pants**	**sight**	**taste**
humor	**parts**	silly	**teach**

40

5-letter words (continued):

teeth	touch	**waist**	**worse**
thank	track	**weird**	would
that's	**tried**	**whale**	**wound**
there	truly	what's	**wrist**
thing	truth	while	**write**
think	**tutor**	**whine**	wrong
those	until	white	you've
threw	**usual**	whole	**yours**
thumb	**utter**	**witch**	youth
times	**veins**	words	
tired	**verse**	world	
today	**vocal**	worry	

Kit Goes Home!

An Easy-Start Reader

Level C, Book 5

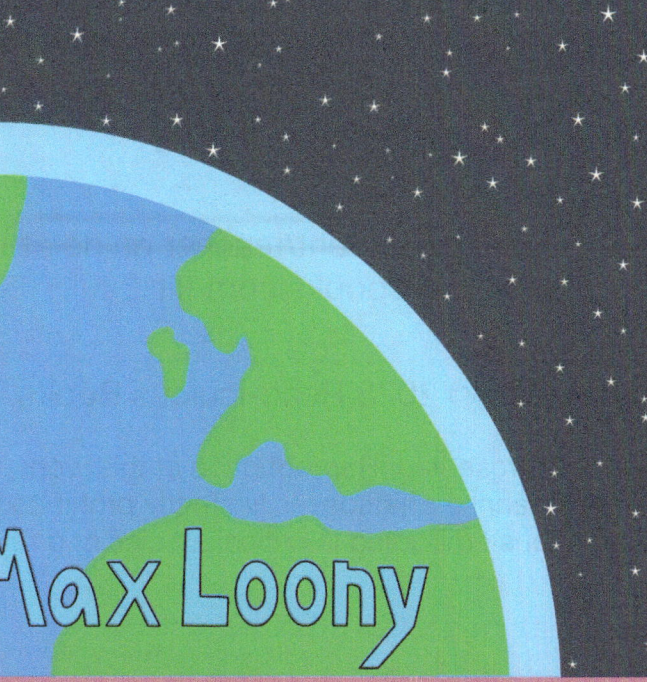

by
Max Loony

Kit Beginning Reader Books

Level C: Kit Is Reading Now

Book C-5: Kit Goes Home!

Written by Max Loony

Concepts in this book*:
- Long sentences, complex rhyme schemes, and more difficult words
- Only short words (1-5 letters)
- Short vowel sounds in various previous patterns
- Long vowel sounds in various previous patterns
- Past-tense, present-tense, or plural words in patterns —*ed* and —*es* said using both one and two syllables
- Vowel-consonant exception sound (*eigh*) with silent *gh*
- Vowel-consonant exception sound (*ough*) with silent *gh* making multiple different sounds
- Many new two-syllable words including new pattern aCC*le*
- A couple new three-syllable words in new patterns VVCVV and CVCVV (*audio, video*)
- A few new short contraction using 5 letters (*hadn't, home's, wasn't*)
- Additional use of possessive words with apostrophes
- Several new phonetic exceptions (*aches, break, broad, dead, doors, earn, gems, heavy, herb, hours, movie, ready, souls, tech*)

*Word Pattern Key: C=Consonant, V=Vowel, *italics*=a specific letter, —(dash)=start or end of word

Download free parent/teacher guide at:
      readiculousbooks.com/kit

Copyright © 2023 Read-iculous Books

All rights reserved. Reproduction of this work, in whole or in part, in any manner whatsoever, is strictly prohibited, except for brief quotations embodied in critical articles and reviews.

BOOK C-5:
KIT GOES HOME!

by Max Loony

Hello there! It's me, Kit!
I had a good visit
To the earth, but now it's time to quit!

I'm going home to rest,
Since I had a good quest,
While in your world I was a guest.

I've known many faces.
I've even been in races—
Like that one with Bob and his son.
I must say, wasn't that day such fun?

The last time I saw Bob,
I asked, "What are you doing?"
His reply was, "I'm going
Off to work, for I got a new job!"

See, I didn't go to earth to earn.
I was only there so I could learn.
And that's why I did bring
All the money I'd need,
So I could live like a king
And my time would be freed!

Back at home I would sit
And think all about it!
So I saved all my wages
For what must have been ages!
I spoke to our old sages
And I read many pages
About Earth and all of its zones.
And I felt it deep down in my bones!

A love in me arose,
And that's why I chose
To check out your world by my self.
And I kept some items for my shelf:
Like a shell and some rocks,
And a pair of new socks,

And some other cool stuff I did buy.
Now, some of this stuff makes me smile,
Since in that place I spent a while,
But some of it does make me cry!

I hadn't just taken a photo.
I got a whole bunch of video!
When I get back home, those I will share.
All of this is proof that I was there!

As a bonus, I'll make a short movie,
Then I'll show it as I tell my story.

One rock I did save
I got near that cave.
I must say, it has got a faint glow!

Just a piece of the earth,
But I think it is worth
Quite a lot! I'm so glad I did go!

It seems like my trip was so brief,
And now what this feels like is grief!

But it's time to go home—
It's not time to play dumb!
So no more will I roam—
Ready or not, here I come!

To fly home, I flick my wrist
And then give these dials a twist.

My world is not the same as this place,
And it's so far away out in space!

The trip home can be rough,
But I, Kit, am quite tough!
On the way, I did cough
Right after I took off.

Ah, so soft is my seat!
Yeah, this ship is so neat!

You know what? Hey, I ought
To show you my cool ship,
So I'll let my robot
Drive me home for this trip!

I said, "I'm a proud owner,"
For my ship is just super!
Yes, it has so much power,
And I have truly loved it
Since the very first hour—
From the very first time that I flew it!

This ship is much nicer
And quite a bit newer
Than the one I first had
Which I got from my dad!

The motor won't break, for it has no gears.
My ship keeps me safe: I don't have any fears!
I trust it, for I've owned it for years.

Even if it flies at an odd angle,
I can still set some food on this table!
I don't float when I go in a door,
For my ship pulls me down to the floor!

Now, I fly with good sense,
But even if I crash,
The ship's sides will not mash
And they will not get any dents!

My ship's so "high tech,"
Even if it does wreck,
It can be fixed easy and quick!

While its speed has no limit,
It still stays very quiet.
It moves all about just like magic!

No, it is not noisy at all!
Its sides are made of soft metal.
I guess that it's some kind of steel.
In any case, it has a good seal
For it keeps the air fresh—
Which I need for my flesh!

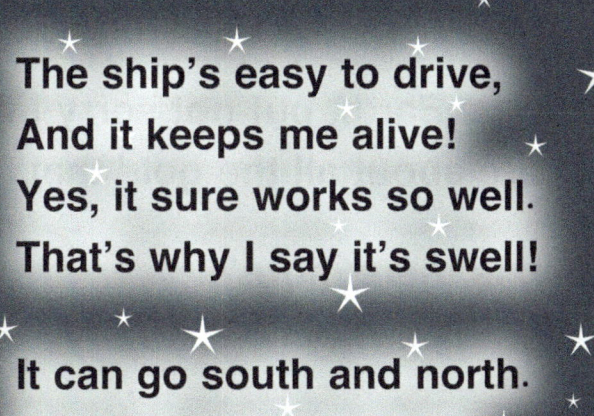

The ship's easy to drive,
And it keeps me alive!
Yes, it sure works so well.
That's why I say it's swell!

It can go south and north.
It can go east and west.
It can go back and forth.
Yes, my ship is the best!

It shows me stars in space,
Then I pick where to go.
To get me to that place,
It kicks in the turbo!

I am sad to leave Earth, but not sorry I went,
And I don't care about all the gold that I spent!

Of my money, is there more?
It's not on this upper floor!

On this level that's lower,
Down here by the ship's motor,
Is a big stack of boxes
With gold coins and gold hunks in all sizes!

In my world, gold is cheap.
I've still got quite a heap,
But I don't truly care.
If you were here, I would share!

Out among the stars of space,
Very swift was my ship's pace!

I knew soon I'd be there,
So I went back to my chair.
I said, "Soon I'll again taste the air
Of my own world that I love,
For I've spent far too long up above!"

The entry was bumpy,
But my ship is so fancy
That it dives right on down like a dove!

In my world, stuff is heavy:
A bit more than on Earth.
To be back I'm so happy,
For this world is where I had my birth!

My world is very flat,
And its hills are all small.
At their tops, I have sat,
And for miles I've seen all!

Some of these hills are fiery
Where the lava flows down!
While the dirt is quite rocky,
Most of it is just brown!

But we also have color
That's quite a bit nicer:
We have reds and blues and some green.
Take a look! You will see what I mean.

Water sits in deep lakes:
Some are hot, some are warm!
Other ones are quite cool.
The warm ones take my aches!
They take many a form.
Each one's like a big pool!

Water comes from below.
These pools can even grow!
All these lakes—we do have so many!
But an ocean? We don't have any!

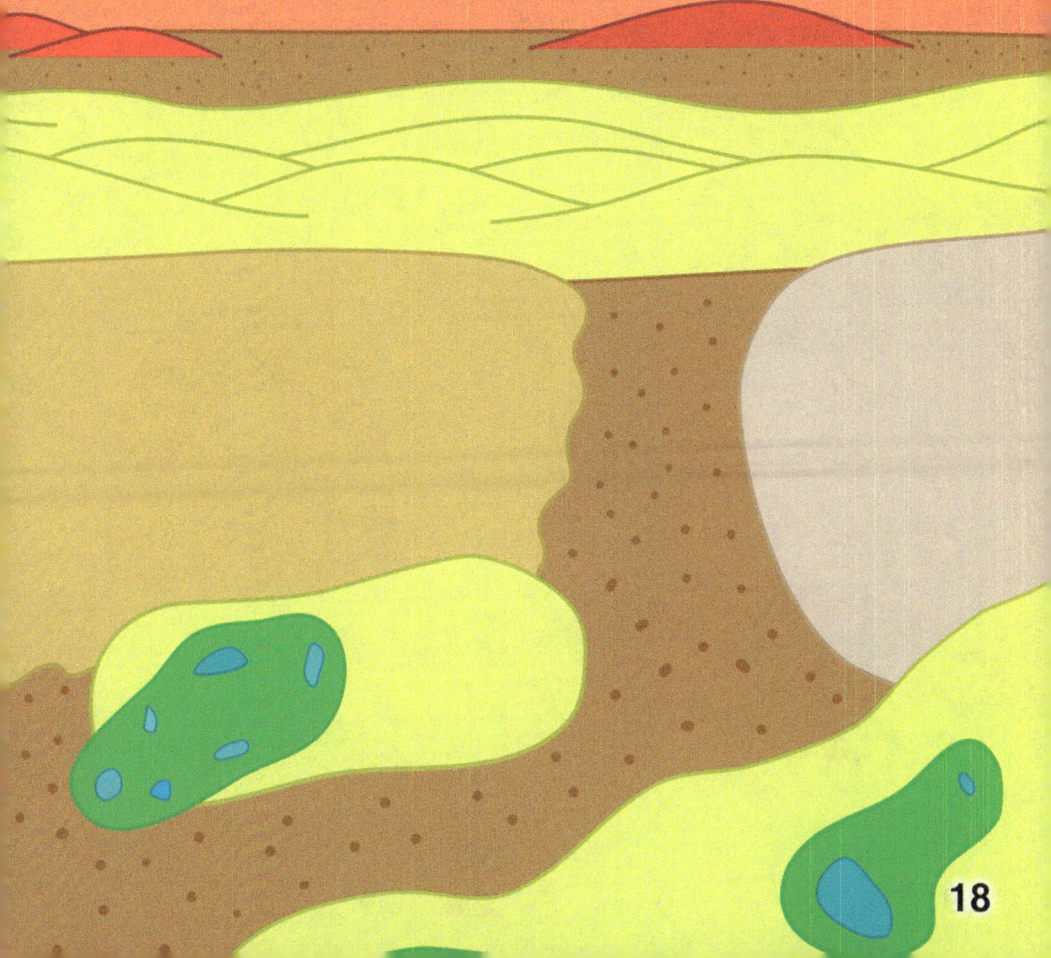

Soon I found my own home:
It's a short and squat dome!
I'm sure it's not like yours.
See the curve in the doors?

In my yard is a patch
Of a plant that's like grass.
Right there is where I catch
Bugs that glow in a glass!

The pool in the back is quite hot.
Oh yes, I like that one a lot!
See my yard? I have no fence there.
But out here, well, why would I care?

My home's in a broad plain
That does not get much rain
In a field with some trees
Where I like to drink teas!

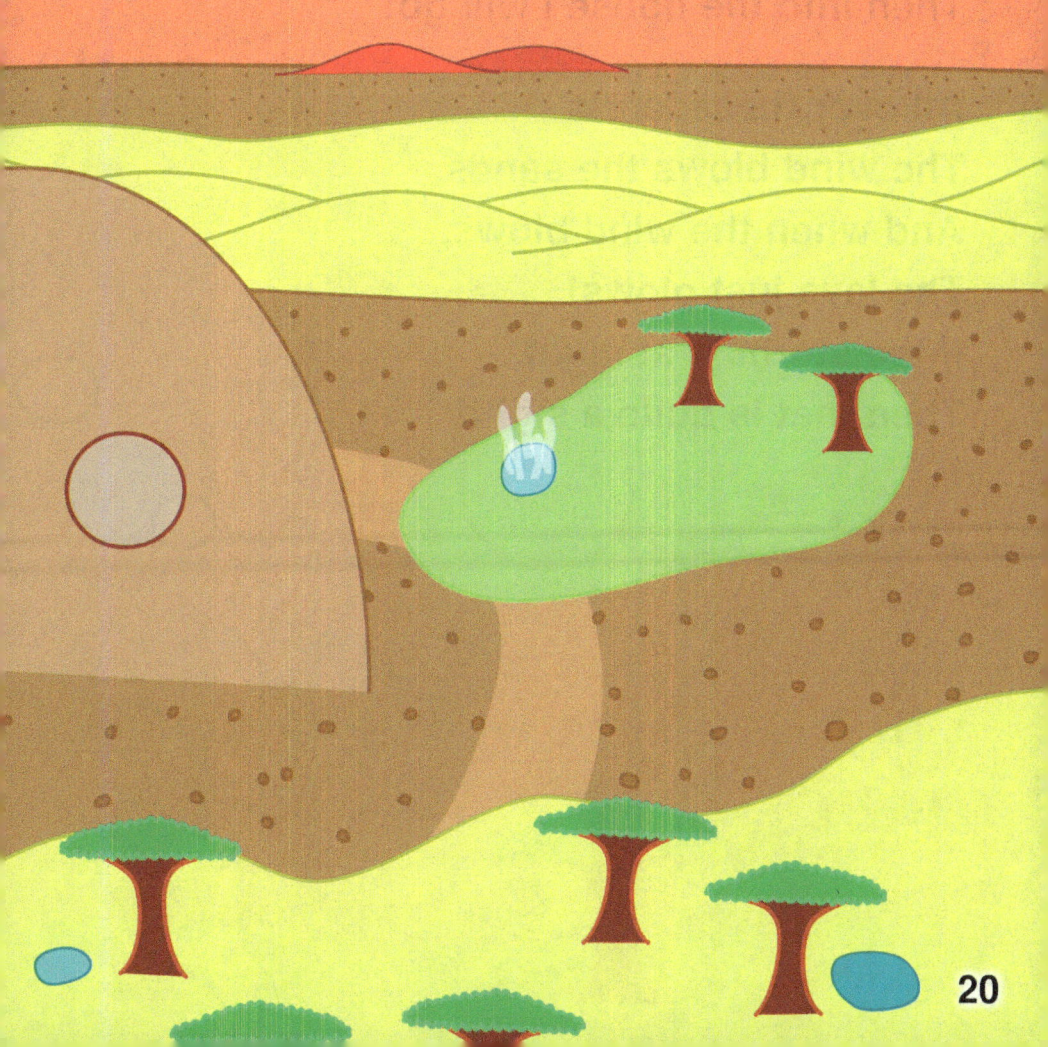

20

No, it's not often rainy,
So I don't have much mud.
But when it does rain,
My land has no drain!
Too easy, it turns into a flood!

And it's not often windy,
But when the winds blow,
They can bring a big storm!
If I want to stay warm,
Then into the house I will go!

All over these lands,
The wind blows the sands,
And when the wind blows,
The lava just glows!
If the storm is at night,
Then that is quite a sight!

You may think it's scary,
But I do not agree.
The air is not toxic!
(This is a good topic.)
It's safer for me!
I don't have any fear,
For I grew up here!

With the dials in my hand,
I'll get ready to land!
My mind's keen and alert
As I park my ship on the dirt.

23

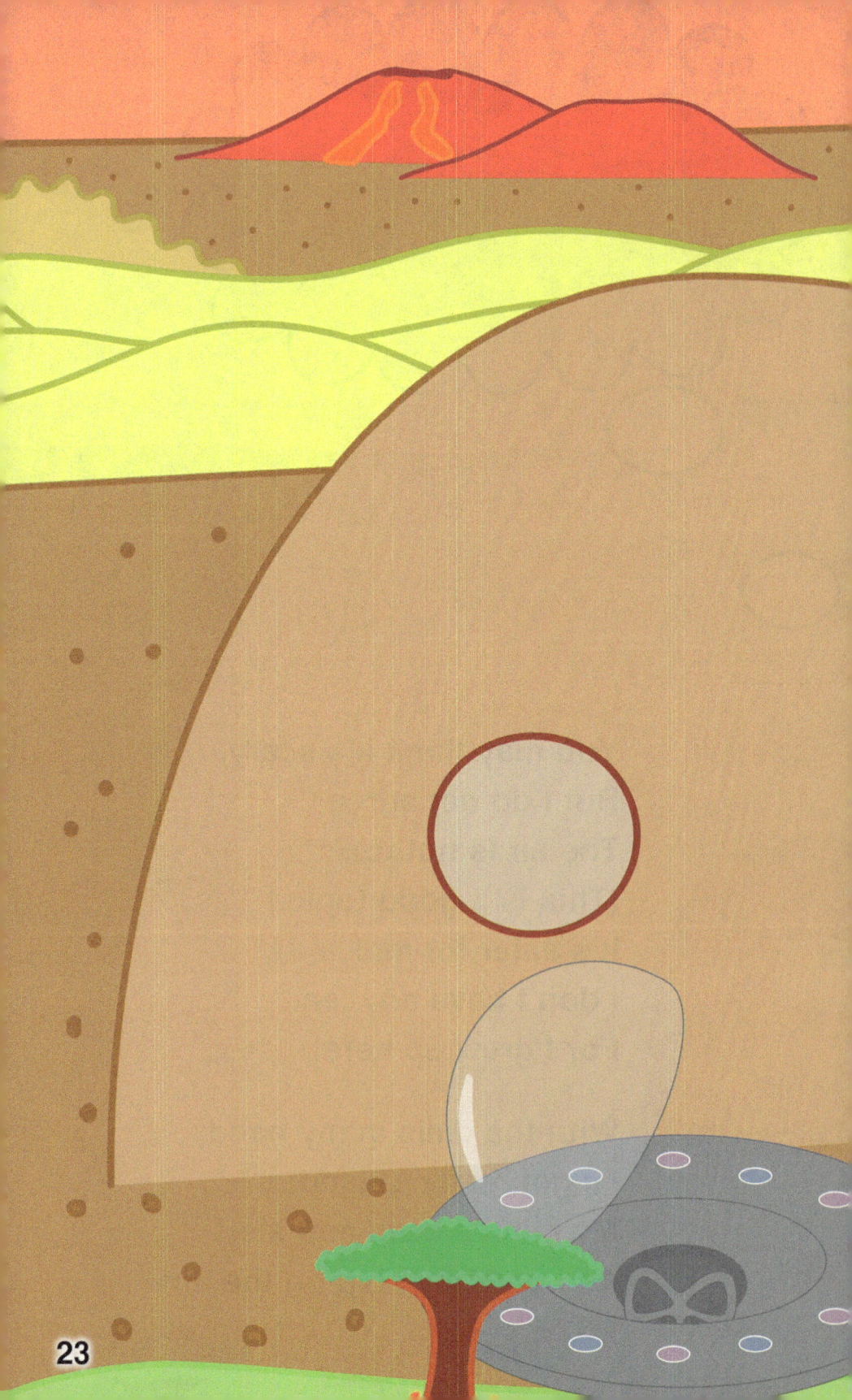

I'll empty my cargo.
This task is kind of slow!
I'll haul boxes and cases
While I make funny faces!

All this stuff that I carry—
Like the goods that I found
And the gold that's so heavy—
I'll pile it all up in a mound!

Now I've got some seed—
It's from Earth, you know—
For I took some home as a prize!

So I've got a need
To see if they will grow
And if a new plant will arise!

Even if these seeds grow,
They might be a bit slow,
For all suns aren't the same:
Ours is like a dull flame!
Do you see how it has a red glow?

Yes, it's big and red.
No, it is not dead!

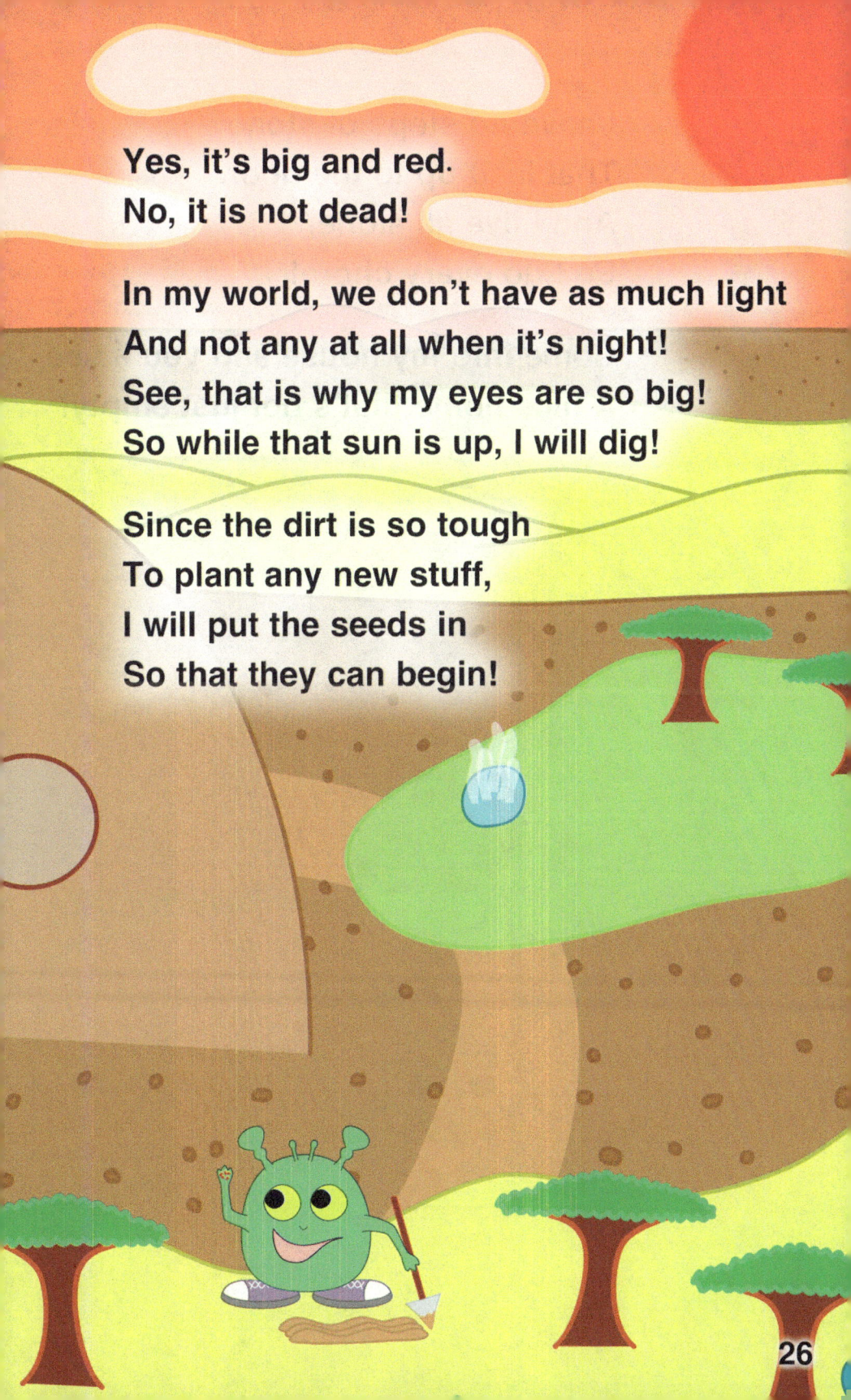

In my world, we don't have as much light
And not any at all when it's night!
See, that is why my eyes are so big!
So while that sun is up, I will dig!

Since the dirt is so tough
To plant any new stuff,
I will put the seeds in
So that they can begin!

I have no steps of stone
That lead up to the door.
And I live all alone,
So I do every chore!

Come into my house and you'll see
A nice home that's not just empty!

No, it is not fancy,
But then it's not messy!
I have a few rooms but no halls.

The edges are round.
There isn't much sound.
It's quiet and clean.
Ah! I like this scene!
See the color of paint on my walls?

When I take a rest from my labor,
I'm among every major color!

29

Home is basic and sweet.
I never allow trash!
I clean up my mash
Right after I eat!

Here's a couch and a table and a stool
And a shelf with books! Isn't that cool?

There are times I play games
With a buddy or two.
I won't tell you their names,
But we never argue!

I wish you could see it!
When all of us play,
It is quite the sight!
We make it our habit
To play games all day
And into the night!

You would see the food that Kit fixes,
And how we all sit and eat mixes!

One of us will keep score
For hours, maybe more!
I'm often the loser of the game.

But it's all just for fun,
Even if I win none.
I don't care! I won't feel any shame!

When I sit all alone,
I make plans to go out.
I don't cry, I don't moan,
And I don't mope about!

But now that I'm back,
I'd like to hit the sack!

"Home sweet home!" I do say,
For it's been quite a day!
Now, I could kick back and just rest,
But I've got to give you your test!

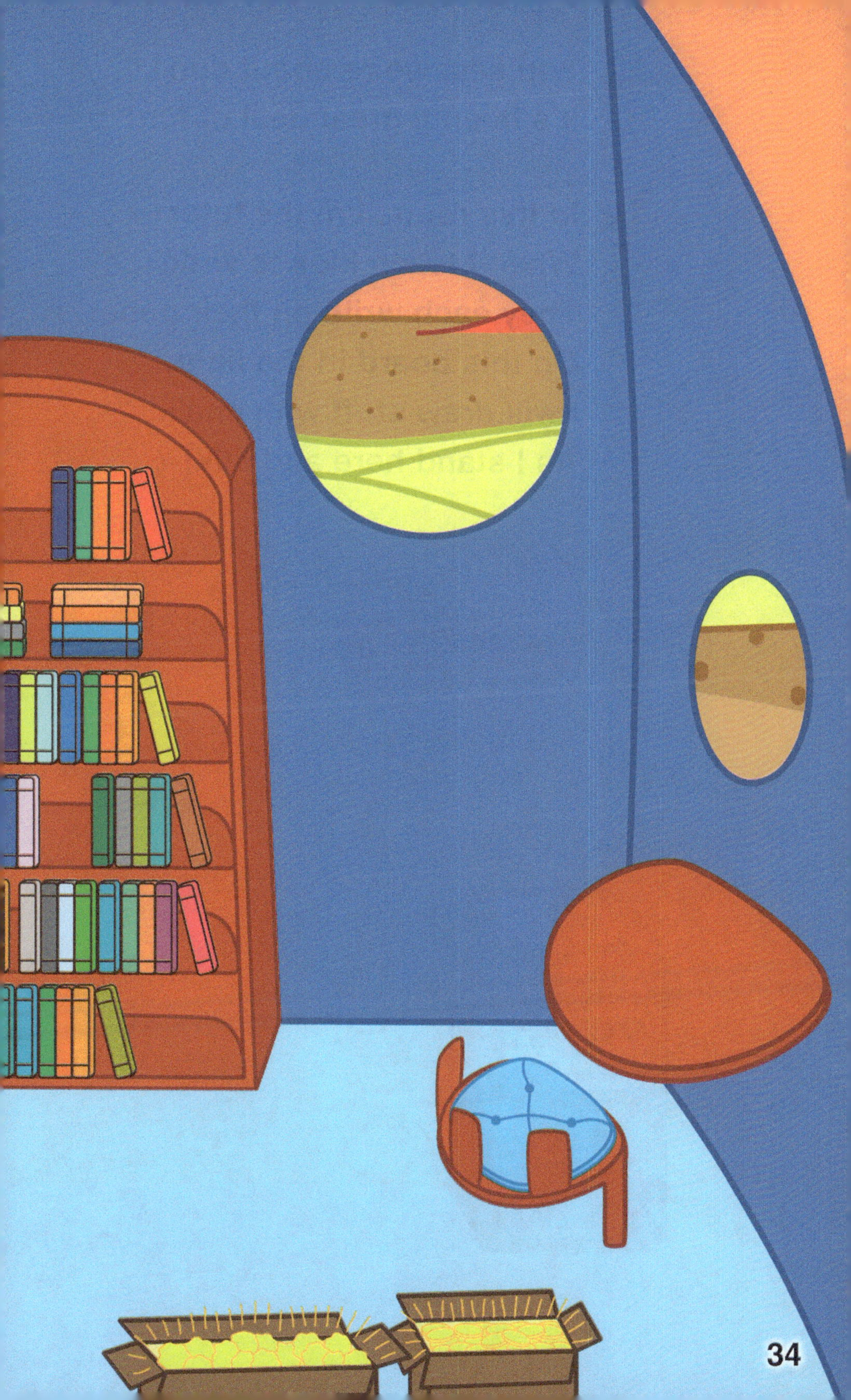

You see, we're about done.
It's been a great deal of fun!

In this room, I'm the tutor
When I teach kids to write.
They each write on their paper.
On this board in the light,
I will draw stuff with chalk
As I stand here and talk!

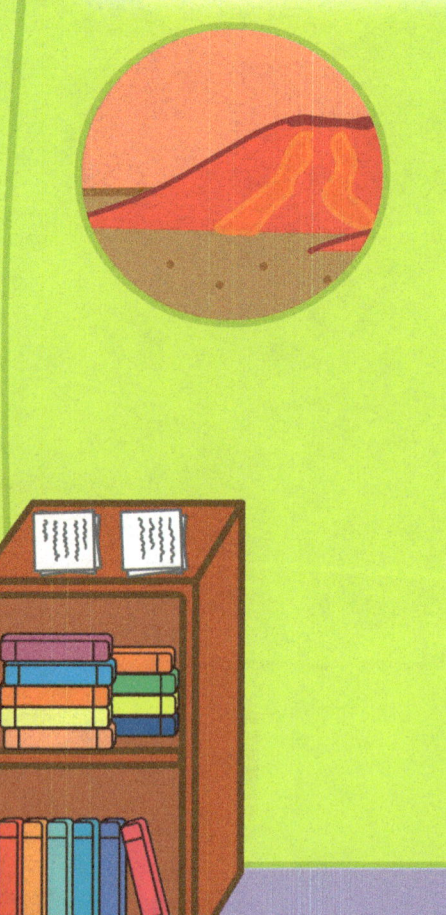

My mind's a clear one,
And I keep it in shape.
I do math just for fun,
And I weigh every grape!

There are eight of them here.
One ounce is their total.
And if it was not clear,
The scale is made of metal.

Let's talk about how
You know how to read now!
It's fast, but at first it was slow.
Okay. Are you ready? Let's go!

I'll get this off my chest,
What I did learn at first:
Some words are the best,
And some are the worst!

The best words are easy
Like: "I'm not as crazy as my tooth!"
The worst we spell badly
Like: "Some girl says their souls might learn truth."

Some words are hard to spell,
But you're doing so well!
You truly can learn it.
Your brain is so quick!
Just keep on doing it,
And it will all click!

Easy Words
I'm not as crazy as my tooth.

Phonetic Exceptions
Some girl says their souls might learn truth.

Some words share a sound,
The same sound at the end,
And what I have found
Is that those words can blend!

When you hear the same sound
    at the end of the line,
This is what we call a rhyme.
If they are only close,
    it's okay, do not whine!
They don't need to be exact,
At least not all the time!
It is just fine, in fact!

"Rhyme" is a weird word all on its own!
It means that we care about the tone.

If a line
Does not rhyme,
Don't think that it's bad—it still works!
And each set of lines we call a verse.

Rhyming Words

sound   end
found   blend
line   own
whine   tone
rhy

I don't want you to miss
That a rhyme works like this:

After I put those seeds in the dirt and got muddy,
I came into the house and I sat down to study!
As long as the sound at the end is the same,
You'll find that to rhyme is a fun kind of game!

You see, I'm very smart!
I read, write, and do math, but I'm not good at art!
I might be a bit vain!
My head is so big since I have a large brain!
Next I'll teach you some more,
For I like doing this: it is not a hard chore!

Yes, I've been a clear guide.
Stick with me for the ride!
It's my job to amuse you,
So I'll try not to lose you!

Verbs
carry
move
drop
amaze
wait
ask

VERBS

Now it's time to go over again
Some ideas that you've been given,
Some facts about words you ought to know by now...

How do you tell apart a weed from an herb?
How do you tell apart a noun from a verb?
I'm sure you can do it, but do you know how?

41

Compound Verbs

have eaten
will do
did look
don't need

Verbs are those words that do some kind of task
Like carry, move, drop, amaze, wait, or ask.
A verb gets stuff done,
A verb can have a tense:
In the past, now, or to come.
Soon all of this will make sense!
Some verbs need two words
   to get done their deed
Like "have eaten," "will do,"
   "did look," and "don't need"!

Let's move on! What are nouns?
   Well, let's take a look!
Real stuff you can touch, like paper or a book.
Any kind of "thing" you can think is a noun,
Like timer and food, pride and joy, rocks and gems,
A motor, a penny, a clock, or a clown,
Also other facts, ideas, or items,
A color, a robot, a job, or a place,
A human or beast, an alien or space!

pride
joy
rocks
gems
motor
penny
clock
clo

facts
ideas
items
color
robot
job
place

44

Prepositions:
above
below
among
over
under
along
aside
upon
near
Adjectives:
rich
poor
soft
rough
mean
gruff
sharp
dull
fine
shiny
round
nice
calm
ADJS.
PREPS.

Some words tell you more about nouns and stuff
Like sharp, dull, or fine, rich or poor, soft or rough,
And like shiny and round, nice and calm,
    mean and gruff!

Some words tell you how one thing is by the other
Like next, near, into, upon, above, and over,
Along, among, aside, with, below, and under!

Some short words have two parts:
Words like begin, story, and photo.
And some words have three parts:
Words like audio and video.

To read words like these isn't much labor:
You just make each sound in the right order!

2 Syllables
be-gin sto-ry
pho-to or-der

3 Syllables
au-di-o vid-e-o

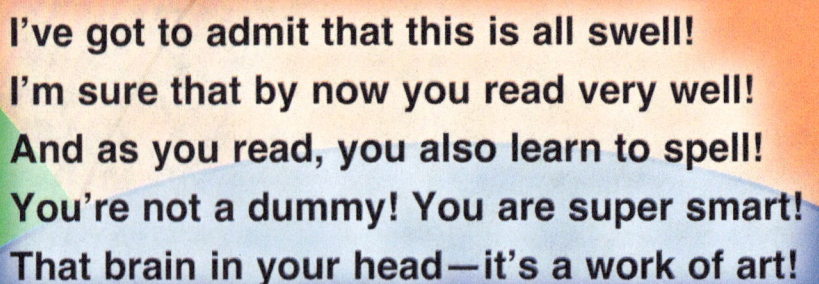

I've got to admit that this is all swell!
I'm sure that by now you read very well!
And as you read, you also learn to spell!
You're not a dummy! You are super smart!
That brain in your head—it's a work of art!

You've grown in your wits!
Now you've got the tools.
In these words of Kit's,
You did learn the rules.

You've heard all my jokes—I've tried to be funny.
I've told you my tales—many a good story.
You've seen me in rain—or out when it's sunny.
You've known how I am—when I've acted silly.
You saw when I dined—with food that was yummy.
You've seen all my gold—yes, it's lots of money!

You've made it this far,
And now you're a star!
That wasn't so hard,
And here's your award:

You know how to read now!
Oh, yes, that will allow
You to learn all kinds of new stuff,
For you know that it's not so tough!

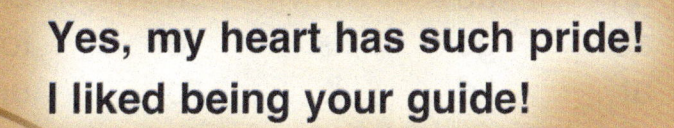

Yes, my heart has such pride!
I liked being your guide!

Well, it's been a great show.
At last, it's time to go!
Wasn't this so much fun?
Hey, look now! You're all done!

The End.

Words in this book (new words are in **bold**):

1-letter words: a   I

2-letter words:

ah	be	I'm	me	on	us
am	by	if	my	or	we
an	do	in	no	so	
as	go	is	of	to	
at	I'd	it	oh	up	

3-letter words:

air	can	get	job	one	son
all	cry	got	joy	our	sun
and	dad	had	Kit	out	the
any	day	has	let	own	too
are	did	hey	lot	put	try
art	dig	his	may	red	two
ask	eat	hit	mud	sad	was
bad	end	hot	new	sat	way
big	far	how	not	saw	why
bit	few	I'll	now	say	win
Bob	fly	I've	odd	see	yes
but	for	it's	off	set	you
buy	fun	its	old	sit	

4-letter words:

ages	been	bugs	care	cool
also	best	call	case	**dead**
away	**blow**	calm	cave	deal
back	book	came	come	deed

4-letter words (continued):

deep	game	kind	must	roam
dirt	**gems**	king	near	rock
does	gets	**Kit's**	neat	room
dome	girl	knew	need	sack
don't	give	know	next	safe
done	glad	land	nice	said
door	glow	last	none	same
dove	gold	**lava**	noun	save
down	good	lead	okay	says
draw	grew	let's	one's	**seal**
drop	grow	like	**ones**	seat
dull	hand	line	only	seed
dumb	hard	live	**ours**	seen
each	**haul**	long	over	self
earn	have	look	pace	ship
east	head	lose	pair	show
easy	**heap**	lots	park	sits
even	hear	love	past	slow
eyes	**herb**	made	pick	soft
fact	here	make	**pile**	some
fast	high	many	play	soon
fear	home	**mash**	pool	star
feel	hour	math	poor	stay
felt	into	mean	**quit**	such
find	isn't	miss	rain	**suns**
fine	just	**moan**	read	sure
flat	**keen**	**mope**	real	take
flew	keep	more	**reds**	talk
food	kept	most	rest	task
form	kick	move	**rich**	**teas**
from	kids	much	ride	**tech**

4-letter words (continued):

tell	time	verb	went	with
test	told	very	were	wits
than	tone	wait	west	won't
that	took	want	what	word
them	tops	warm	when	work
then	trip	we're	will	yard
they	upon	weed	wind	yeah
this	vain	well	wish	your

5-letter words:

about	arise	brain	clear	drain
above	arose	**break**	click	drink
aches	aside	**brief**	clock	**drive**
acted	**asked**	bring	close	**dummy**
admit	**audio**	**broad**	**clown**	earth
after	**award**	brown	**coins**	eaten
again	badly	buddy	**color**	**edges**
agree	**basic**	**bumpy**	comes	**eight**
alert	beast	bunch	**couch**	empty
alien	begin	**cargo**	**cough**	**entry**
alive	being	**carry**	could	every
allow	below	**cases**	**crash**	**exact**
alone	birth	catch	crazy	**faces**
along	blend	chair	curve	**facts**
amaze	**blows**	chalk	**dents**	**faint**
among	blues	**cheap**	**dials**	fancy
amuse	board	check	didn't	**fears**
angle	**bones**	chest	dined	feels
apart	**bonus**	chore	**dives**	fence
aren't	books	chose	doing	field
argue	**boxes**	clean	**doors**	**fiery**

5-letter words (continued):

first	guest	level	north	quiet
fixed	guide	**light**	**nouns**	quite
fixes	habit	**liked**	ocean	**races**
flame	**hadn't**	limit	**often**	**rainy**
flesh	**halls**	lines	order	**ready**
flick	happy	**loser**	other	reply
flies	heard	**loved**	**ought**	rhyme
float	heart	**lower**	**ounce**	right
flood	**heavy**	magic	**owned**	**robot**
floor	**hello**	**major**	owner	rocks
flows	here's	makes	**pages**	**rocky**
forth	hills	maybe	**paint**	rooms
found	**home's**	means	paper	**rough**
freed	**hours**	messy	parts	round
fresh	house	**metal**	patch	rules
funny	human	might	penny	**safer**
games	**hunks**	**miles**	photo	**sages**
gears	ideas	**mind's**	**piece**	**sands**
given	items	**mixes**	place	**saved**
glass	**jokes**	money	plain	**scale**
glows	**keeps**	**motor**	plans	scary
going	**kicks**	mound	plant	scene
goods	kinds	moves	**pools**	**score**
grape	known	**movie**	**power**	seeds
grass	labor	**muddy**	pride	seems
great	**lakes**	names	prize	sense
green	lands	never	proof	shame
grief	large	**newer**	proud	shape
grown	learn	**nicer**	**pulls**	**share**
gruff	least	**night**	quest	sharp
guess	**leave**	noisy	quick	shelf

5-letter words (continued):

shell	**steel**	three	**wasn't**
shiny	steps	**timer**	water
ship's	stick	times	**weigh**
short	still	tools	weird
shows	stone	tooth	where
sides	**stool**	**topic**	which
sight	**storm**	**total**	while
silly	story	touch	whine
since	**study**	**tough**	whole
sizes	stuff	**toxic**	winds
small	sunny	trash	**windy**
smart	super	trees	words
smile	sweet	tried	**works**
socks	swell	truly	world
sorry	swift	**trust**	worst
souls	table	truth	worth
sound	**taken**	turbo	would
south	**tales**	**turns**	**wreck**
space	taste	tutor	wrist
speed	teach	**twist**	write
spell	**tense**	under	**years**
spent	that's	**upper**	you'll
spoke	their	**verbs**	you're
squat	there	verse	you've
stack	these	**video**	yours
stand	thing	visit	yummy
stars	think	**wages**	**zones**
stays	those	walls	

All books in the *Kit Beginning Reader Books* series:

Level A: Kit Learns To Read
Book A-1: Meet Kit
Book A-2: More Kit
Book A-3: Kit Does Math
Book A-4: Kit And Critters
Book A-5: Kit Meets People
Book A-6: Kit And The Bug

Level B: Kit Reads Some More
Book B-1: Kit Comes To Town
Book B-2: Kit Takes A Drive
Book B-3: Kit Goes Hiking
Book B-4: Kit Shops For Clothes
Book B-5: Kit Reads About Animals

Level C: Kit Is Reading Now
Book C-1: Kit Explores A House
Book C-2: Kit Goes Out To Eat
Book C-3: Kit Explores The Earth
Book C-4: Kit Loves Life!
Book C-5: Kit Goes Home!

Kit Beginning Reader Parent/Teacher Guide

(Books are available individually or combined as 3 volumes for Levels A, B, and C.)

Made in the USA
Coppell, TX
12 November 2023